The POWER Series

Desert Storm
GROUND WAR

Hans Halberstadt

Motorbooks International
Publishers & Wholesalers

To the men and women who died in the desert,
especially Major Marie Rossi, US Army.
And also to my dear friend and altered ego,
Vera Williams

First published in 1991 by Motorbooks International
Publishers & Wholesalers, PO Box 2, 729 Prospect Avenue,
Osceola, WI 54020 USA

© Hans Halberstadt, 1991

Motorbooks International books are also available at
discounts in bulk quantity for industrial or sales-
promotional use. For details write to Special Sales
Manager at the Publisher's address

Library of Congress Cataloging-in-Publication Data
Available
ISBN 0-87938-561-8

On the front cover: The M1 Abrams main battle tank
proved to be virtually invulnerable to Iraqi tank fire.
Several M1s received direct hits, but none were destroyed.
Department of Defense

On the frontispiece: An Iraqi tank destroyed in the battle
for Khafji. *USMC*

On the title page: An M1 tank silhouetted by the setting
sun. *Hans Halberstadt*

On the back cover: A Cobra attack helicopter launches
missiles toward its target. *Hans Halberstadt* Upper inset,
Sp. Shannon Segall brandishes a captured Iraqi rifle.
Kirby Lee Vaughn Lower inset, a destroyed Iraqi tank.
USMC

Printed and bound in Hong Kong

Contents

Acknowledgments

A salute to all who contributed to telling this story, particularly: Lt. Col. John Baptiste, S-3, 197th BDE, Lt. Col. Raymond Barrett, Commanding Officer, 3rd/15 INF 24th ID, Lieutenant Colonel Raymond Cole, Ops Officer, I MARDIV, Col. Andy Dulina III, FORSCOM PAO, CWO Randy Gaddo, USMC Public Affairs Office, April Halberstadt, Col. Richard M. Hodory, Commanding Officer Task Force Papa Bear, Col. Randolph House, Commanding Officer, 2nd Brigade 1st Cav, Col. Rick Kiernan, Army PAO Media Branch, Lt. Col. Dave Marlin, Commanding Officer 4/37 Armor, 1 ID, GySgt. Dave Marriot, I MEF PAO, Lieutenant Colonel Meyers, Commanding Officer Task Force Sheppard, Capt. Joseph Molofsky, USMC advisor to Saudi 10th Brigade, Maj. Rick Rife, 1/3 AVN (Attack), Colonel Rokas, Commanding Officer 325 PIR, Captain Sutherland, Commanding Officer B/3rd/15 INF, Vera Williams.

Preface

The problem with history—for both readers and writers—is that a complete and fully accurate picture of any event in the past is impossible. History books are notorious for the inclusion of lies, errors of fact, omissions of crucial detail and bias. That said, here is a history of Operation Desert Storm that probably includes all of those, plus a few others. This book is part of the story of the war, the dramatic part. It emphasizes the story of what soldiers call the FEBA, the Forward Edge of Battle Area where the guns fire and the blood (usually, not always) flows.

The *whole* story of the war in the desert couldn't fit in a squadron of these volumes. More than a million people participated directly, if you include both sides. Many millions had their lives affected. Twenty-eight nations deployed forces to the coalition side. It was an immense congregation.

So the intent of this book is to give you a taste of the time—a narrow but detailed impression of what some of the people involved saw, heard, thought and did. I've stressed the role of the combat arms: the infantry, artillery, armor, and attack aviation. This is a collection of war stories from primarily US sources. It omits the Iraqi version of events. Missing, sadly, are the war stories of the Arab units that fought bravely and well.

I have collected the experiences of a hundred or so soldiers and let them tell the story. Most saw combat. Some moved fast and far, others only a few kilometers. Most not only fought, but were out front, leading the charge. Some were tank drivers, gunners and riflemen—young enlisted soldiers and Marines who saw their battles through their weapon's sight systems. Others were the commanders, officers with an overview of a whole battalion's experience and role in the battle. In between were many platoon sergeants, lieutenants, and captains with another set of impressions. I asked all to do two things: tell what their unit *did* and tell what they *felt*.

One interesting thing I noticed was that people remembered different things about the same event. Sometimes the information from one person conflicted with that from another. Sorting it all out was not easy. Some of my data may conflict with other published data. For example, lists published by several sources are inconsistent about the spelling of the names of Americans killed in action.

So this is an incomplete account of the Desert Storm ground war, leaving some things out, putting extra emphasis on some things at the expense of others. There's some of my bias in here, too, but at least I warned you about it. That's history for you.

Hans Halberstadt

Introduction

What a strange, interesting, *surprising* war this was. Wars are always, I suppose, an odd, theatrical, emotional experience for those taking part and those watching as well. This was a strange one. Even the people who fought it say so.

The business of shedding blood—your own or that of others—has a curious place in our culture, both attractive and repellent. It's sometimes a dreadful, dreary, ghastly thing; war can also have moments of humor, heroism, and great pageantry. It's the kind of experience that brings out primitive qualities in individuals, good and bad. I've seen valor in battle, and I'll never forget it. A soldier's business is high theater, low comedy, an art, a science, a secret society with odd rituals and old traditions, a mixture of the most primeval emotions and the latest technologies. No wonder it fascinates us so.

I've been watching and writing about the US Army for the last six years and about the Marine Corps somewhat less. Before that, I served in the Army, and played a little combat role in Vietnam as a machine gunner on helicopters. I have a personal and professional interest in the Army that goes back a long way. And I've always wondered, along with my friends in the infantry, armor, artillery and aviation communities, how it would all work, if push came to shove. We all wondered about the weapons, the doctrine, the aircraft, the tactics and occasionally, about the people involved. Would the Apache really work? Would the missiles hit? Would the Bradley fail or fight? Enquiring minds wanted to know. But, even more, would Americans ever support their armed forces again, after the hostility of the public toward the military following Vietnam? We wondered; then we found out.

In the summer of 1990 the armed forces community was isolated and rather alienated from the larger society by a twenty-year tradition of mutual hostility. Many Americans believed then that the armed forces were a refuge for the incompetent and ignorant, that the weapons systems were expensive trash, that with the demise of the Warsaw Pact and Soviet imperialism there was no longer a real need for a large military anymore. Americans wanted their peace dividend, and they wanted it now.

The war in the Persian Gulf region caught the armed forces, along with the rest of us, a little emotionally unprepared. The sudden invasion was a surprise. The strong, unified response, by the United States and the United Nations, was itself a surprise. The rapid deployment, so smoothly executed, wasn't the disaster Pentagon critics had been predicting but an efficient success story. The firm stand taken by the president, Congress or the UN had the courage and commitment to take a stand and stick to it. That just hasn't been our tradition.

For two decades our newspapers and magazines have been criticizing the weapons and the soldiers in the armed forces. According to reports, our military was a gang that couldn't shoot straight. Although the soldiers and Marines didn't share the low esteem for their compatriots and weapons presented by the news media, they also couldn't avoid noticing a lack of confidence, either.

So they planned and trained and tried to look into the crystal ball to prepare for whatever the future might hold. Their training was changed, made tougher and more realistic. Few in the armed forces had any idea how well trained they were until they put the training to work in the desert. Many have said their training was tougher than battle. They were also surprised at how well the equipment worked, under the worst possible conditions. Things that failed in training worked in combat, like Murphy's Law in reverse. People that failed in training worked in combat, too. One commander told me that there was not a single incident in his company during the whole six months that warranted even minor disciplinary action. As he said of his company's experience: "These guys performed beautifully! All the commo worked—unbelievable! All the weapons systems were operational—unbelievable! Everybody maneuvered perfectly—and *that* was unbelievable."

Another surprise was that the tactics and strategy of the battle planning was delegated to the professionals instead of being done by the politicians. This is a new, positive and successful lesson of this war. Vietnam was planned in a different way.

The AirLand Battle Doctrine worked when actually employed; the surprise here was that it was employed against the massive, Soviet-style forces for which it was designed.

Of course, everybody was surprised at the feeble, ineffective resistance shown by the Iraqis. We all heard for months how tough they were, how battle hardened, how well equipped, trained and supplied, how they were going to inflict tens of thousands of casualties on us in battle, and with unconventional weapons. Instead, they rolled over and played dead—or were dead. I thought we'd take thousands of battle deaths ourselves, and so I think, the troops did as well. Iraq had promised we'd "swim in our own blood," and we wondered if they might be right.

Does that mean that Iraq's capabilities were vastly overrated? I don't think so. Instead, the rapid, efficient victory of the coalition was the result of two basic factors: Iraq's failure to continue into Saudi Arabia, and a good plan well executed on our side. Iraq could have kept Kuwait had its forces taken the ports and airfields of northern Saudi Arabia, but they didn't. And once the forces and the will to use them were in place, the AirLand Battle ground down Iraq's military machine. The elements of AirLand Battle were perfectly designed to deal with this kind of threat, making it look easier than it really was.

Until this war, strategic air power had never really delivered on its promises to make a real difference on the outcome of a war. This time was different, and nobody will ever question the role of air power again. The planning and execution of the air phase of the campaign is certainly the prime reason the ground campaign was so successful. Air power didn't win the war, but it made the war quicker, easier and safer for the coalition than it would have been otherwise. Air power eliminated the enemy's ability to resupply, to communicate, and even to move, making them hungry, confused and scared. No wonder the Iraqi soldiers were ready to quit at the first opportunity.

The reaction of the American public to this conflict was not what I expected, either. I really thought we would have escalating protests and a lot less support for the troops. Instead, the protestors were shouted down. I'm still not sure why, and neither are some of the military people I know. As one said, "I'm just waiting for all the pseudo-patriotism to die down so we can get back to normal."

Well, maybe he'll get his wish. But I think a lot of people, in many nations, have learned some lessons and Americans will have more affection and respect for its soldiers, sailors, airmen, marines and Coast Guard personnel for a long time to come.

The ground war lasted about a hundred hours, depending on when you start counting. Within those hundred hours, and with the weeks of battlefield preparation that preceded them, several transformations occurred. Operation Desert Storm changed the way the world community of nations deals with the tradition of one nation invading its neighbor. The war changed the way Americans think about those who serve in its military. The war changed the way the armed forces of the United States think about themselves.

This book tells the story of the ground campaign through the experiences of those who fought it, from the beginning on 2 August 1990, to the formal ceasefire in March of 1991. Half a million people participated on the coalition side, from many units. Including everyone was obviously impossible. Therefore, I've included the accounts of units across the front, from the two large corps that raced across 250 miles of enemy territory on the west, to the Marines who moved much more slowly and fought much harder on the east.

Chapter 1

Warning Order: 2 August to 16 January

The Pentagon, Midnight 2 August

If you wear the right badges, the guards will let you in to the Pentagon, then down Corridor 8, Second Floor, B Wing, past more guards and the cypher locks, to the National Military Command Center. This is the cerebral cortex of the entire US armed forces establishment, where the nerve fibers end, where the reports come, where the decisions begin. When things go bad anywhere in the world, this is where the senior American intelligence analysts try to figure out what is really happening and what—if anything—the United States needs to do about it. In the early hours of this sultry August morning, things are very bad indeed.

For the past several weeks military analysts have been looking at imagery from the HK–11 spy satellite showing the northern Persian Gulf area. The roads and highways of southeastern Iraq are thronged with tens of thousands of military vehicles, all headed for the border with neighboring Kuwait. These images, with a variety of communications intercepts and eyewitness reports, show a major build-up of forces from Iraq's huge army massing along the border with its small neighbor to the south, the emirate of Kuwait. The build-up could be an empty threat, part of the political posturing in that part of the world. It could also be the preparations for a real attack. To the intelligence staff studying the pictures it was difficult to tell.

For many units, the build-up and training during Desert Shield was as rigorous as the combat during Desert Storm. Here Cpl. Andy Hodnik, Bravo Company, 27th Engineer Battalion, shows how dusty an engineer can get during training. Kirby Lee Vaughn

Although a threatening move, this build-up alone is neither unusual nor terribly serious. Many nations around the world communicate with their neighbors by demonstrating military power without actually applying it.

Out of the mainstream of world news in mid-summer 1990, Iraq and Kuwait have some differences of opinion, but nothing that seems serious enough to start a war.

Iraq wants $13–15 billion from Kuwait for allegedly stealing oil from under their common border. Iraq wants its little neighbor to also forgive $10 billion in loans provided during the war against Iran. There is a disagreement about the border, and a demand for the use of two islands in the Persian Gulf. There are other demands, but nothing particularly new.

Within the American intelligence community, the equation just doesn't add up to invasion. Analysts from the Central Intelligence Agency (CIA), Defense Intelligence Agency (DIA) and the State Department all conclude that, although the military components for an invasion are in place, the political conditions suggest a threat rather than an actual assault. There are a few individuals predicting invasion, but the consensus is that it is all bluff.

But at 0200 local time 2 August, Iraq's army moves across the border in force. Squadrons of the elite Republican Guards in Soviet-built T–72 main battle tanks, BDRM and BTLB armored personnel carriers, scout cars, Hind attack helicopters, and thousands of infantry sweep down the six-lane highway from the north. Kuwait's tiny army and air force are surprised, but they stand, fight short, violent engagements, and are overwhelmed. At 0530, just more than three hours after crossing the border, the fight for Kuwait City begins. Tanks work into the city block by block while MiG fighters provide air cover.

The emir's brother dies in battle near the royal Dasman palace, with hundreds of soldiers and civilians, but the fire-fight slows the attackers just enough for many to escape down the road to Saudi Arabia. The emir is taken across the border by helicopter. The battle for the capital is over by 1400 and Kuwait City is secured. The invaders press on toward the border with Saudi Arabia, brushing the light defenses aside with minimum casualties.

A-4 Skyhawks from the Kuwaiti air force manage to get airborne and make strikes on the invasion force, but when it rapidly becomes obvious that the invasion is successful they fly to safer havens to the south. By the end of the day Saudi air traffic controllers at Hafir

Al Batin and King Kalid Military City clear thirty A-4s to land. But neither the Kuwaitis nor the Saudis feel safe. There is nothing to stop the attack from rolling south, down the six-lane highway from Kuwait City, to Khafji, Al Jubail or Dhahran, seizing the rich oil fields on the way.

Eight time zones to the west, in the US National Military Command Center and throughout the upper levels of government, the mood is grim for Vice Admiral Jerimiah and the other officers and officials in what they call the Tank. This invasion is more of a threat to the United States than another routine invasion of one nation by a neighbor.

Kuwait is a small, alien culture, far away, but its links to the economy of the West are strong. The loss of its oil production to a renegade nation like Iraq is a

A Heavy Expanded Mobility Tactical Truck (referred to by the troops as a HEMETT) comes off a ship in Saudi Arabia. Heavy resupply vehicles like this made the plan *work. Without the fuel, food, ammunition, spare parts and other essentials the rapid moves over long distances would have been impossible. US Army*

problem of strategic danger to the economy of the United States. But there is a lot more at stake.

If Iraq is able and willing to seize Kuwait, then it probably can do the same to Saudi Arabia. And with the control of that much oil production, Iraq will suddenly become a dominant force in the world economy. That would be bad enough, but what makes matters worse is the Iraq record of unprovoked aggression, sponsorship of worldwide terrorism, use of chemical warfare, plus a vigorous effort to develop nuclear weapons for use against its neighbor Israel. Iraq has a million men in its army, many recent veterans of combat against Iran during an inconclusive eight-year war. Iraq has the fourth-largest armed force in the world, having invested much of its vast oil revenues in the latest military technology available from the Soviet Union, France, Germany and many other nations. Iraq has not only hardware and manpower, but experience and training. It is considered expert in defensive tactics, having learned the principals from the Soviets and practiced them for eight years against the Iranians.

But in the command center the issues for Vice Admiral Jerimiah and his planning cell on 2 August are more basic: What is really going on, and what military response—if any—can the United States realistically offer? As the hours wear on, the answer to the first becomes clear: the complete occupation of Kuwait, and to the second, for the moment, nothing. There is nothing to do but watch and wait.

It is over quickly. While the Iraqi assault elements finally pause to rest that evening, things start to click in the Pentagon where it is still early morning. First the Joint Chiefs of Staff (JCS) are briefed, then the president.

The United Nations holds an emergency session and condemns the invasion. President George Bush freezes the billions of dollars of Iraqi and Kuwaiti assets, then bans trade with Iraq. And the secure telephone and telex lines begin to get a workout.

Although the president makes the final decision to actually use the armed forces in defense of the country, he gets lots of advice from a small group called the National Command Authority (NCA). Included are Chairman of the JCS Gen. Colin Powell, Secretary of Defense Dick Cheney, National Security Advisor Brent Scocroft and President Bush. On 2 August they begin what will be five full days of meetings that will ultimately transform the American armed forces. Behind the NCA, 1,600 people on the Joint Staff begin designing a phased deployment that will—if the decision is actually made—use available

ships and aircraft to project power into the Persian Gulf region.

The problem for them all is that Iraq is more than just another Third World nation. It is fairly prosperous, with a well-educated and large middle class. It has substantial oil revenues that have allowed industrial as well as military development. But much of its wealth has been invested in its armed forces: 1 million soldiers, 5,500 tanks, more than 500 combat aircraft, 3,700 artillery tubes, missiles and rockets, with an unknown number of chemical and possibly nuclear warheads. Much of this equipment is high quality, including Mirage fighters and Exocet missiles from France, Chieftain tanks from Britain, T-72 tanks, Mi-24 Hind attack helicopters, MiG-29 Fulcrum fighters from the Soviet Union, land mines from Italy and the G-5 artillery piece from South Africa.

And all this combat power has been massively, violently applied against Kuwait, whose armed forces have only 275 tanks, 36 elderly combat aircraft, 90 artillery pieces and 18 helicopters at the beginning of 2 August. By sunset little of that remains.

Warning Order to the 82nd Airborne

One of the first calls goes to the Army's 82nd Airborne Division's parent, Headquarters, XVIII Airborne Corps. Two hundred miles south of Washington, in the steamy center of North Carolina, is the Army's Fort Bragg, home of the 82nd Airborne Division, XVIII Airborne Corps, and other military units. If the Pentagon is the armed forces' cerebral cortex, places like Fort Bragg are its muscle and bone.

Bragg is a big place, with lots of room to practice the art of war. Paratroopers jump from airplanes here virtually every day. Green Berets train here, and Fort Bragg is home to some of them, too. The ultra-secret, ultra-elite Delta Force calls Bragg home; it trains behind barbed wire and high earth berms and operates out of guarded compounds. Bragg is a big, busy place.

Right next door, for the convenience of these units, is Pope Air Force Base, home to the C-130 and C-141 transports that get the 82nd Airborne in the air. The Air Force is an essential part of the mission for the units at Bragg. When a mission is launched, the response is always based on available airframes.

The 82nd is a special division, the only parachute division in the American Army. It has a glorious history, with many battle honors from World War II and since. It was one of the heroes of the Normandy invasion. The 82nd has a reputation that includes a willingness to bleed.

The 82nd Airborne today has a special role in American military planning. It has the responsibility to be first to go to an emergency, anywhere in the world, on order from the National Command Authority. Like a fire department, about a third of the division's 12,000 men and women are always on alert, a responsibility that rotates among the brigades. The soldiers carry beepers off duty and don't stray far from home telephones. And when called to action, they have no more than eighteen hours to get the lead aircraft "wheels up" and on the way to trouble. So, on 2 August, as on any other day, the rucksacks and parachutes are packed, vehicles are loaded with ammunition and weapons, and people are waiting for the phone call that will send them down to Green Ramp and aboard the big aircraft.

The Army's 82nd Airborne Division Ready Brigade (DRB) is the alert force with the eighteen-hour responsibility. Notification will put them on the ground on the other side of the world about thirty-six hours after the call is made to send them. But, as the planning and intel staff in the command center know well, the DRB is a light infantry force hardly able to defend itself against the massed armor of the Iraqis. On the night of 2 August, the DRB is the 2nd Brigade. The 4th Battalion, 2nd Brigade, 325th Parachute Infantry is on highest alert, the Division Ready Force first to deploy.

The DRB has about 4,000 soldiers, all paratroopers, with their personal weapons and some light, crew-served anti-armor TOW and Dragon missile systems, plus mortars, 105-mm. artillery and the Sheri-

Fresh off the boat, an M109 self-propelled howitzer joins the thousands of other tracked and wheeled vehicles in Saudi Arabia. The M109 looks like a tank, but isn't. Its armor will protect the crew from artillery fragments and machine gun bullets but that's all. But the 155-mm. gun will shoot a 100-pound projectile about twenty miles. US Army

dan armored reconnaissance (recon) vehicle. The Sheridan looks like a tank, but its armor is thin and the vehicle is no match for even the oldest true tanks in the Iraqi force, the ancient Soviet T-55s. But, for the moment, it will have to do.

The 82nd Airborne gets an "execute" order from the National Command Authority, sending the DRB to Saudi Arabia. The eighteen-hour clock starts ticking.

The first call goes to the 82nd Airborne's commander, Maj. Gen. James Johnston, the notification the Army calls a warning order. But neither he nor his planning staff really need it; the news on the Cable News Network (CNN) has already provided a warning that the services of the paratroopers might be required. In times of worldwide crisis the 82nd Airborne's staff doesn't wait for formal orders to think about what may be required. Behind the locked and guarded doors in the plans and operations section in the 82nd's headquarters at Fort Bragg, the staff is already working on the requirements for a Persian Gulf deployment.

The DRB alert roster is pulled out and late in the evening people are told to report in to their company areas. There's nothing unusual in this for the 82nd Airborne soldiers; it's a routine that happens frequently as part of the training routine. But there are usually clues that inform the paratroopers if the alert is just another false alarm or the real thing. And to Captain Rennebaum, commander of an anti-tank company, it comes indirectly: "I was notified about 2330 that evening. My wife was talking to a friend on the phone who called to see if I'd been alerted. She woke me up and I called in. By the time I got into the company, thirty percent to forty percent were already assembled. Guys were taking weapons down to the motor pool, getting ready to go. We got an alert that we were to upload the Stinger missiles; this was for real, not a training exercise. Orders were coming

A heavy mortar team sets up for training. USMC

down, maps being issued, we thought that this was it! When we hit the ground, there was going to be action. We thought we were going into combat!"

The captain and his troops don't get to call home to say goodbye, they just climb onto the aircraft and go. Grenada and Panama kicked off this way. Without being told, their families know this is for real and that their soldiers may not be back for a long time—if they come home at all.

Captain Rennebaum's unit may have a critical mission if the Iraqis attack soon, so he goes with the lead aircraft. It is a long, tense, worrisome flight.

Captain Rennebaum remembers: "I was on the lead aircraft, with the advance party, including General Timmons and the division staff, Colonel Rokas, the brigade commander, plus representatives from all the other battalions to coordinate the arrival of the follow-on units. We were camouflaged up, we had ammunition, we were ready to go into combat. We weren't sure what we were getting into."

The 82nd has one simple, essential and dangerous mission: they will secure an "airhead" for the follow-on forces. If the airfields are lost, the war is lost before it begins. If the airfields are held, a build-up of forces can begin. With enough time, a creditable force can be accumulated and the enemy attacked, but until then two things prevent disaster: Iraqi hesitation and the 82nd Airborne.

For years the Army and Marine Corps have competed for missions, each claiming the rapid deployment role. The current policy makes the Army, with its 82nd Airborne Division, responsible for immediate reaction. The 82nd is deployed by air, either parachuting or airlanding on their objective. Their mission is to be on the way to trouble no later than eighteen hours after the order is received. That makes them highly dependent on the Air Force, which must deliver them by parachute or to a secure airfield.

Although the 82nd can be delivered just about anywhere, they are a light infantry force, vulnerable in some important ways. The Marines offer a complementary ability: they are slower to arrive, but less vulnerable once on the ground. The Airborne offers speed, the Marines offer muscle. It's a good combination in a crisis.

US Forces on Alert

The heavy muscle, on 2 August, is not far away. Only 2,500 miles from Kuwait, a fleet of MPS–2 ships ride at anchor off the island of Diego Garcia. Aboard are all the tanks, artillery, ammunition, fuel, food, medical supplies, tents, communications gear and vehicles an entire Marine Expeditionary Brigade needs for a thirty-day encounter with an enemy force. All the National Command Authority needs to do is add people, and the Marines can be in business within a matter of days.

The Marine mission is similar to the 82nd's, but not quite so rapid. Marines secure beaches and ports, then bring in tanks and artillery by sea. Their response is slower, but their punch is heavier.

On 2 August, the 1st Battalion of the 7th Marine Regiment is completing a three-week training period in the rugged southern Sierra Nevada mountains near Bishop, California. Their training is supposed to conclude with a thirty-five-mile forced march through the mountains. Instead, the battalion is abruptly ordered back to home station at Twentynine Palms to prepare for possible overseas deployment to a desert hot-spot. The Marines are used to heat: their home station is one of the hottest places in the United States. As an operations officer recalled, the word was: "Get ready to go. We don't know *when*, but if we do deploy it will be soon." And so it is.

As 2 August concludes, units throughout the American armed forces are considering what to do if they are called to war. They do this automatically, whenever crises occur that could require American action, but many believe that this particular incident

Pfc. Rocky McKenzie dries his wash on an improvised clothesline in Saudi Arabia. Kirby Lee Vaughn

may actually get them deployed. At the 101st Airborne in Kentucky, the 24th Infantry Division in Georgia, and many other units, brigades, and divisions staff sections stay up late doing "what if" exercises. It is their job to be prepared for rapid reaction to events like the invasion, and they take it very seriously. "I had staff duty the day of the invasion," says Capt. John Sutherland from the 24th Infantry Division, "and the brigade staff was working late that night on contingency plans to get us over there. The unofficial alert was out on the 2nd; the official notice came on the 7th."

Alerts are supposed to be pretty secret procedures, but Captain Sutherland's spies prepared him for the middle-of-the-night call: "Matter of fact, we kind of knew what time the phone calls were coming; I had my alarm clock set so I could be awake and have a cup of coffee at three in the morning when they were gonna tell me to come in and get going."

At about the same time, the president and the National Command Authority tell a lot of other people to get up and moving, too.

3-7 August

On 3 August, the president deploys the command ship *LaSalle* with a task force of missile frigates and cruisers, with more on the way. A carrier battle group centered on the *Independence* moves to the Gulf of Oman.

On 6 August, the United Nations imposes worldwide economic sanctions against Iraq. President Bush orders a military response: Forty-eight Air Force F-15s head for Saudi Arabia with weapons and the authority to use them. The 82nd gets its "execute" order.

On the next day the 7th Marines receive their deployment order and the regiment's preparations go into high gear. The same day, the Army's 24th Infantry Division, with its 216 M1 Abrams tanks, gets the word, too, and things get serious for many people in many units.

The 82nd will be first on the ground, but the Marines will be right behind them. The 7th Marine Regiment has a lot of work to do before deploying to a potential combat zone. Each Marine's equipment, inoculations, power-of-attorney, will and other essentials are checked and verified. The headquarters staff and many others begin working eighteen- and twenty-hour days. For them the problems are intense and acute: instead of a simple regiment, the 7th Marines suddenly grows to a regimental combat team. This means adding an infantry battalion to the three

already present, plus a company of Light Armored Vehicles (LAVs) and tanks. The 7th Marines are now 8,000 strong, nearly the size of a small division, with a total of ten additional subunits to care for and command.

After days of frantic activity and little sleep, the units are formed up in the middle of the night and bussed out the gate with as much secrecy as possible—which isn't a lot. Within a couple of hours the Marines are deposited in a hangar at Norton Air Force Base, California, then loaded onto civilian contract airplanes, huge 747s and DC-10s. Soon they are alone with their thoughts, trying to sleep during the long flight east. On one plane a rumor begins to circulate: the Iraqis have attacked into Saudi Arabia and the 82nd Airborne has been destroyed. Although it isn't true, many of the Marines expect to have a fight on arrival. There is the usual confusion and uncertainty that goes with war. Ammunition is issued to the Marines of the 7th in case they have to fight on arrival. Most land not knowing if the airfield at Dharahn is secure or not. As one marine remembered, "We were prepared for this to be a major problem, just getting off the aircraft, so everyone went with a combat load of small arms ammunition."

"We didn't know what to expect, where we were going," said one platoon leader. "But I knew I was in trouble when the door of the airplane opened and this teenager from the Air Force came up the steps wearing a t-shirt, and *drenched* in sweat. I was wearing a helmet, flack jacket and full combat equipment; I took two steps outside the aircraft and it was like I was in a shower. It was pretty nasty—and it didn't get any better, either."

It takes two days for the entire regiment to arrive, 15 and 16 August. Until the vehicles and weapons systems arrive, there isn't much to do except worry and sweat. It is even too hot to sleep. The rumor now is that the Iraqis will attack soon, but the Marines will have eighteen to twenty-four hours' warning before being hit. There is a frantic search for TOWs and other anti-armor weapons, but few are found.

For a week the Marines live and work in conditions many consider worse than combat. Daytime temperatures are well over 100 deg. Fahrenheit, with high humidity. There is no air conditioning in the warehouses where they are billeted, no showers, no toilets other than a few portable toilets that quickly overflow. There are no bunks or anything else to sleep on except for scrounged sheets of cardboard to pad the concrete floor. The heat and noise makes sleep for those off duty nearly impossible, even in the middle of the night when it cools off to only 95 deg. Anything cooler than air temperature becomes known as "Saudi-cold," even if it is 100 deg.

But the Marines know this is more than another exercise; the Iraqi army is only an hour or two up the road. In spite of the adverse conditions, they accomplish something amazing: the regiment is fully launched within only seven days of notification, and defensive combat patrols begin operating only nine days after that. Tanks and artillery are out in the field, with combat loads of ammunition and a job to do, only a couple of days later. Ten days after arrival the 7th Marines have two battalions of artillery, their armored amphibious vehicles (AAVs), their mechanized infantry and a reinforced tank battalion operating around the essential port city of Al Jubail.

Enemy versus Friendly Capabilities

In the days and weeks that follow a sequence of decisions is made in Washington, in the United Nations and in the capitals of many nations around the world. Nearly all the world's nations support the embargo that is swiftly dropped on Iraq. Even the Soviets, long friends and supporters of Iraq, condemn the invasion and side with the United States. On 8 November President Bush deploys another 200,000 troops and Marines to the Gulf, bringing the total to 400,000. Two US Navy battleships, six aircraft carrier battle groups and numerous smaller naval vessels take up patrol stations in the Persian Gulf and Red Sea. The Air Force and Marine Corps set up shop at Saudi air bases at Dhahran, Tabuk, Hafir Al Batin, Yanbu and Riyadh, and start air operations with F-15E and AV-8B fighters, F-111 bombers and a mixed bag of supporting players.

Politics and diplomacy are far from the minds of the few American Marines and soldiers already on the ground. For the 82nd Airborne's paratroopers, it's a matter of self-defense around the airport at Dhahran. The 7th Marines' First Battalion, meanwhile, sets up shop north of Al Jubail in a sunny spot they call Cement Ridge. They dig defensive positions in the relative cool of the night, try to sleep during the day, and wonder when the enemy attack will begin. Their job will be to provide a little time for those further back if the attack does occur, but nobody has any illusions about how long they'll last against a major armored assault. The Marines and soldiers of the 82nd Airborne begin referring to themselves as "speed-bumps."

The Pentagon and operations staff have a tremendous problem. Iraq has lots of modern equipment, tons of ammunition, a horde of people, excellent training and perhaps most important, lots of recent battlefield experience. The Iraqis are considered masters of Soviet-style defensive tactics. They are known to possess, and have used, chemical weapons. They are believed to have nuclear weapons technology, and perhaps some kind of weapons available for use. Their supply line is short and secure; ours is long and—if the airfields at Al Jubail and Dhahran are lost—extraordinarily vulnerable. Their population is wildly supportive and unified behind the invasion of Kuwait.

It quickly becomes obvious, too, that within the Iraqi army is a hard-core organization with special missions, extra trust and responsibility, the best weapons and a formidable record of accomplishment: the Republican Guard Corps, sometimes known as the Presidential Guards. The Republican Guards have the best equipment, extra pay and independent leadership. Three Republican Guards divisions lead the charge into Kuwait (two are armored) and they all function as a unified corps. They are organized with more flexibility and variety than American units of comparable size.

A headquarters element from the 2nd Armored Cavalry Regiment sets up shop somewhere in the desert. The tracks are M577 variants on the good old M113 armored personnel carrier. The M577 carries lots of radios, commanders, and the unit coffee pot. In the foreground is a Humvee tricked out with a removable communications system. US Army/Sp. Fass

Intel reports indicate two major Iraqi headquarters: the 1st Subcorps Group commands two armored divisions, the 1st Hammurabi and the 2nd Medina, the 3rd Tawakalna Mechanized Division and 4th al-Faw Motorized Infantry; the 2nd Subcorps Group headquarters commands the 6th Nebuchadnezzar and 7th Adnan Motorized Divisions already in Kuwait, plus the Republican Guards 5th Mechanized. Iraq's twenty special forces brigades appear to be part of these commands, adding a highly competent light infantry force for deep penetration missions, able to operate alone or in concert with the heavy units. It is known that the Republican Guards stress a mobile assault, supported by Soviet-built Hind and French-built Gazelle attack helicopters using HOT anti-armor missiles. They claim about 500 of Iraq's 1,000 modern main battle tanks, mostly Soviet T-72s, plus about 1,000 BMP infantry fighting vehicles.

Allied Combat Power, Late Summer

To oppose the Republican Guards the United States first sends the 82nd Airborne, the lead elements of the DRB landing at Dhahran on 7 August. Their first mission is to defend the air base north of the city to establish an airhead. This is a critical mission because the security of the airfield will allow follow-on forces to arrive close to Kuwait. Tens of thousands of soldiers, hundreds of vehicles and all kinds of weapons systems start arriving at Dhahran, reinforcing the airhead.

The 7th Marine Expeditionary Brigade is followed by hundreds of other units, regular and reserve.

The Pan-Arab forces also worked to prepare for combat. Here, Arab armor crewmen replace a power pack on one of their tanks. USMC

Combat units from around the world get their orders and move out. The Marine's 3rd Aircraft Wing, with FA-18s and AV-8B fighters, and CH-53 heavy-lift helicopters follow from El Toro and Tustin, California, and Yuma, Arizona. They are shortly followed by the 1st MEB based at Kaneohe Bay, Hawaii, and the 4th MEB from Norfolk, Virginia.

The Army's 1st Corps Support Command follow the 82nd Airborne to help set up shop in the desert. Their lead elements arrive by USAF C-5s and quickly

Military Units

Half a million Americans went to the Gulf, but they didn't go as individuals; all were members of *units*. These units all have names, most of ancient origin. They are traditional structures for organizing soldiers and employing them in battle. And there's an interesting thing about these units: they are like families, collections of bonded individuals with a collective identity and allegiance. It's been truthfully said that a soldier fights for his buddies and will die for them. Many marines and soldiers risked their lives for the well-being of those in their units, and some lost the gamble.

Squad

The squad is the smallest basic unit in a ground organization. Marines have thirteen men in their version, the Army includes eleven. In both cases a junior sergeant is in charge, but the Marines say he is the *commander*, the Army makes him the squad *leader*.

There are two fire teams in an Army squad, with five riflemen on each team, and one machine gunner for the squad. When the squad attacks, one team moves forward while the other provides covering fire. Marine infantry companies contain three fire teams of four men each.

Platoon

An Army platoon is built from four squads; the Marines use three. Both add an officer, who either leads or commands, depending on whose platoon it is. A radio operator and a platoon sergeant are added, too, plus several others (medics, and so on).

Platoons can attack fairly substantial objectives. With about forty-five to fifty men, a full-strength infantry platoon can move across the battlefield in bounds, part over-watching and protecting, the other part bounding forward under cover of their friends. In the defense, a platoon can hold about a quarter mile of terrain—its squads and fire teams arranged to provide mutual support.

Company, Troop (Cavalry) and Battery (Artillery)

The company is the basic unit of the ground forces, with two or more platoons and a typical strength of about 120 soldiers or Marines. The commander is normally a captain, assisted by an executive officer (a first lieutenant) and one additional officer (a second lieutenant) to lead or command each platoon.

Marines use a different model than the Army for their company. A Marine infantry company, for example, will typically have three platoons (three squads of thirteen each), a weapons platoon (mortar, machine gun and antitank squads), plus a command squad including the commander, executive officer (XO), first sergeant and supporting players like the radio-telephone operator (RTO).

Companies in either branch are named with letters of the alphabet, always expressed using the international phonetic version. There is usually an Alpha, Bravo, and Charlie company in every battalion. There is often a Delta as well, and that will be a weapons company in the Marines or an antiarmor company in the Army infantry.

A company should be able to defend about 300 meters of line.

Task Force

A task force is a special, temporary collection of different kinds of units for a particular mission. In Desert Storm, these task forces usually included infantry, who are essential for clearing bunkers, rough terrain, trenches; armor, for brute force, long range, speed and protection for the infantry; artillery, which can reach out and put suppressive fire on enemy positions at long ranges, preparing the battlefield before the force arrives and supporting the attack once battle is joined; and attack aviation, a kind of flexible, rapid, aerial artillery. The Marines built large task forces—Taro Ripper, Papa Bear, and the others—to breach the Iraqi obstacles and move on Kuwait City. Each includes a command, ground, air and logistic support element.

OpCon

Operational Control; another way to say attached. The 82nd Airborne Division was *OpCon* to the French 6th Light on day one, then were *chopped* to go north on their own.

Chopped

It is common for one unit (platoon, company, and so on) to be taken from its parent organization and sent off to reinforce another unit or to execute an independent mission alone. When this happens, the people involved may say they've been chopped to do something.

A variant is cross-attached, which involves trading different kinds of pure combat organizations (infantry, armor, artillery, anti-tank) and inventing a hybrid. This is what the 24th Infantry did on its long move north, by adding a tank platoon to a mechanized infantry company, and chopping one of the infantry platoons to the tanks. The results are called company teams, or task forces.

Battalion

Battalions consist of two or more companies, plus other assets, usually about 1,200 people. A lieutenant colonel commands a battalion.

Battalions are always numbered, often in confusing ways. A Marine will say he's a member of "one-seven"; it's your responsibility to know that he means, 1st Battalion, 7th Marine Regiment. Likewise, one of the voices in this text came from the commander of "Delta, 1st of the 325"; that's Delta Company, 1st Battalion, 325th Parachute Infantry Regiment. Since Delta would be the fourth company in the battalion, you are expected to infer that he commands the antitank specialists for the battalion.

Brigade

The Army and Marines use this term for quite different organizations. The Marine brigade is always an Expeditionary Brigade, and is equivalent to a small Army division. It differs from an Army brigade in that it is designed to be independent, with its own ground, air and logistics organizations. You can plunk a Marine Expeditionary Brigade (a MEB) down just about anywhere on the face of the earth and it will wreak death and destruction on the forces of evil all by itself (if necessary) for up to sixty days. There are about 8,000 Marines in a MEB.

Officially, an Army brigade is two or more battalions, but is nearly always three, plus assorted extras (artillery, armor, scouts, engineers, and so on), about 4,000 strong. A brigade is commanded by a full colonel (Army) or general (Marines).

Regiment

Less than an Army division, more than an Army brigade, the regiment is a unit that is difficult to define. Again, the Army and Marines do different things under the same name.

A Marine regiment is rather more like an Army division in size, scope and function. The 7th Marine Regiment included about 8,000 people when it deployed to the Gulf—not much smaller than one of the Army's lighter divisions.

A regiment is an ancient military formation, an important bit of history for many. In Britain, the regimental tie is an old tradition. In Britain and in the United States as well, soldiers and marines often develop a life-long identity linked to service with a particular regiment.

Division

A division consists of two or more brigades (or Marine regiments) with supporting units. The Marine version tends to be much larger than the Army's. 1st and 2nd Marine Divisions in Desert Storm were both over 18,000 strong; the Army's 82nd Airborne only had about 11,000.

Divisions are big business in the conflict resolution department, always able to operate independently and usually able to make things happen by themselves. As big as they are, divisions can (and have) been destroyed in a single day during heavy fighting. When a division commander makes a mistake, he can kill thousands of his own people—something that has happened with great frequency in military history.

Corps

A corps is two or more divisions operating together under one commander. There were two major corps operations in Desert Storm: XVIII Airborne and VII, coordinating the movements of many thousands of people at the same time. A corps attacks or defends a huge amount of real estate, depending on terrain and other factors; in Desert Storm, VII Corps was spread over a hundred miles of front, and after a few days of assault stretched hundreds of miles back into Saudi Arabia.

begin preparing for company. In temperatures that routinely hit 120 deg., the 1st Corps soldiers begin setting up tents, servicing vehicles, erecting shelters for radar, medical, supply, administration and all the other functions a large fighting force requires.

Then comes the 197th Infantry Brigade, an independent mechanized infantry unit from Fort Benning, Georgia. The 197th brings M1 tanks and Bradley armored fighting vehicles (AFVs) to reinforce the 82nd Airborne's light infantry resources. Now there is a chance of at least slowing an attack by the Iraqi forces only four hours up the highway.

The 197th deploys at the end of August after a frantic few weeks. The brigade is the biggest separate brigade in the Army, with lots of M1 tanks and Bradley AFVs, all of which have to be prepped and uploaded with ammunition. The soldiers arrive in Saudi Arabia on 30 August and 2 September; the hardware arrives a month later.

Within a few days the 197th is mounting combat patrols in the desert near Al Udayliyah, with the 24th Infantry Division, the first heavy unit in the country. They begin an intensive program of training and acclimatization. Part of the training involves converting from the older M1 tank to the newer, up-gunned M1A1. The brigade also receives a weapon that will later become very useful, the M19 machine gun. The M19 has been part of the Marines' inventory for many years, but is new to the Army. The weapon shoots 40-mm. grenades with great accuracy to ranges over a mile. There are also hundreds of trucks, huge HEMMETT resupply vehicles, engineer equipment and all the rest.

The heat was a problem for the 197th, as for all the early arriving units, but it wasn't a surprise. As one soldier remembered, "We trained early in the morning, took a siesta for three or four hours in midday, then trained again later in the afternoon when it was cooler. We also started training at night, until we were acclimatized. And it worked out well; our battalion didn't have any heat casualties at all."

After days of intense preparation, the 24th Infantry Division is assembled and with elaborate security precautions marched off to a holding area where hordes of local news media teams record everything for the evening news. The units are penned in the holding area for a week. "We spent a week uploading ammunition into the vehicles," says Captain Sutherland. "Trucks were coming in from all over the country; the roads were backed up with trucks loaded with ammunition. We drew over a million dollars worth of ammunition in a day!" For units accustomed to meager allotments of training ammunition, the sudden generosity is a shock. But if the Bradley IFVs are to be worth anything in the desert, they must be ready to go when they come off the ship, and each gets a combat load of 25-mm. rounds for the chain gun and many get TOW missiles, too.

The 24th arrives at the end of August and quickly deploys into the desert as Task Force Smith. Says one soldier, "We set up a brigade defense, waiting for the other brigades to show up. Delta Company, along with 2/4 Cav set up a mechanized screen; their mission was to be visible."

Sergeant Haynes is of the platoon sergeants from Delta, and he and his four Bradleys' first mission was deception: "Part of our mission was to move our vehicles all around, tanks and Bradleys, to different locations along the highway where anybody could see them. We only had a company—and the tanks weren't working at the time—but our mission was to be visible." The idea is to make the Iraqis think there is more to oppose them than is actually available. And, for whatever reason, it seems to work.

Initially, the rules of engagement prohibit having rounds chambered. The tankers fire only if absolutely sure that they are about to be hurt or killed. Sergeant Haynes: "The rules of engagement were really pretty good. You had to have a solid, military target, and if you pull the trigger, you better kill it. Answer with overwhelming firepower; a sniper gets a 120-mm. tank round."

"We tried to prepare for the heat by drinking two gallons of water on the plane, till everybody was ready to explode. We got there in the middle of the night, got loaded onto the busses for the Chinese fire drill to get us over to the port. That bus ride was probably the most dangerous thing we did the whole time we were over there. The Saudi bus drivers were racing each other to see who was going to be first."

Settling into a Routine

From September through December, the 24th, along with most of the other units, settle down into a routine that seems to many just like that back at home station: training, exercise, routine maintenance, plus the necessary security patrols. It is boring for the young soldiers who still don't know what the generals are planning. For many the long, empty days are oppressive. Morale declines with inactivity and rises with training exercises and preparation. One soldier remembered: "There were all kinds of rumors—that we'd go home on a certain date, then the day would arrive and a new rumor would replace it. The invasion was going to be in November, then

December...the rumors were more fun than anything else. They kept you guessing."

As the thousands of soldiers and their equipment start flooding into northern Saudi Arabia, the 82nd Airborne soldiers are far forward, providing some measure of security. It is a vulnerable moment. If the Iraqis attack now, in force, the situation could be extremely desperate. The 82nd is a light force, without real tanks to oppose the enemy's T–72s. Instead, they field the light Sheridan, a recon vehicle that is light enough to be dropped from an aircraft. The 82nd anti-armor defense will depend on TOW and Dragon missiles fired by soldiers who know they are expendable. It is a sobering thought for Captain Rennebaum and his TOW missile platoon members: "At this point we thought the Iraqis would cross the border into Saudi Arabia, so 2nd Brigade went forward and started looking at positions to defend from. This was going to be it. At that point we were the furthest northern deployed US forces. People realized it could happen at any moment.

"The infantry guys weren't going anywhere. If they were overrun they would have died in place. My guys would have been able to fire, move, fire again. We would have lived to fight again, but these infantry guys, Alpha, Bravo, and Charlie companies, they were dug in deep and it was understood that they weren't going anywhere."

When the 82nd first arrived they were, as one trooper put it, scarcely more than speed-bumps for any serious invasion of Iraqi armor. The 24th's tanks and light armor, along with another 12,000 soldiers, added more steel to the defense; now there was a stop sign.

By mid-September, with the build-up going full blast, the 7th Marines are now operating as a mobile counterattack force in an area near the coast, an intersection of roads called the Triangle. Here they

Two soldiers from the 24th Infantry Division mine the beaches of Saudi Arabia. US Army/Gil High

are poised to hit the flanks of an anticipated Iraqi thrust to the south. With other Marine elements now in place and conducting patrols and defensive operations, they have a name: Task Force Ripper.

The 3rd US Army's headquarters started arriving. The 11th Air Defense Artillery Brigade from Fort Bliss added their Vulcans, Stingers, and Chapparal air defense systems to provide countermeasures if the Iraqi air force elected to try attacks on the growing air- and beach-heads along the Persian Gulf. The 3rd Armored Cavalry Regiment, the "Brave Rifles" from Fort Bliss, Texas, with a heritage for valor 140 years old, arrived with more tanks, Bradley armored fighting vehicles, and troops. Then the 2nd Armored Division, from Fort Hood, and their neighbors the 1st Cavalry, arrived with them. The 101st Airborne, the fabled "Screaming Eagles" from Fort Campbell, Kentucky, who discarded their parachutes in favor of helicopters fifteen years ago, arrived, too, set up their tents, and began to practice the air assault mission that is their specialty.

A squad of infantry from the 82nd Airborne patrol the northern portion of Saudi Arabia during the early months of the build-up. For a time they were all that stood between the essential ports and airfields and the massed Iraqi armor only a few hours' drive to the north. US Army

Politics and Diplomacy

While all the military preparation is going on, the real battle is at the United Nations and in the headlines. Iraq makes a series of rather odd proclamations and gestures. They take thousands of foreigners hostage and threaten to use them as human shields. They threaten the use of unconventional weapons against any attack. They promise to attack Israel if hostilities begin. They promise to inflict hundreds of thousands of casualties; we will, according to them, "swim in our own blood." Kuwait is declared to be Iraq's nineteenth province.

On 29 November the United Nations issues a virtual declaration of war, a resolution authorizing "all necessary means" to eject Iraq from Kuwait after 15 January. After an emotional debate, the US Congress authorizes the president to conduct offensive military operations in support of UN resolutions.

About half of all the coalition ground force is American, the rest from a grand coalition of nations. The crisis inspires a kind of cooperation that hasn't been seen since World War II, if then. There are twenty-eight partners in the alliance, many from the Gulf region: Saudi Arabia with 40,000, Syria commits 19,500, Qatar sends several thousand, Egypt sends 38,500, and even 11,500 exiled Kuwaitis take up arms. Czechoslovakia sends 225 to help with chemical warfare decontamination. From Pakistan come 11,000, Bangladesh sends 2,000, and even 310 mujahedin show up from Afganistan.

The British send 30,000 of their best, including the 1st Armoured Division with squadrons of excellent Chieftain main battle tanks, scout cars, troop carriers and thousands of some of the world's most professional soldiers. Among many others deployed are the famous 4th and 7th armoured brigades—the Desert Rats who earned immortality in World War II. From ships and aircraft arrive four squadrons of Royal Scots Dragoon Guards, the Queen's Royal Irish Hussars, the 1st Battalion of the Staffordshire Regiment, plus artillery, engineers, medical, communication and transportation units, and more.

France contributes 12,600, including the 7,600 from the 6th Light Armored Division, Foreign Legionaires, and fighter aircraft. The French AMX-30 tank is lighter than the main battle tanks of the British and Americans and has a good gun and excellent crews.

Over the weeks and months the forces build in an amazing process that sometimes looks like precisely managed chaos. Five thousand tanks, half a million people, their food, fuel, vehicles, mail, weapons, ammunition, communications systems, spare parts for everything—it all gets packed, shipped, unloaded and sorted out at the bases and the ports on the other side of the world. Professional soldiers and marines from many units and many nations are formed up in platoons, companies and battalions, are ordered to attention and are marched off to war. Reservists in their forties, fifties, and even sixties also receive their orders, trade suits and ties for battle dress uniforms and helmets, air conditioned offices for a 120-degree sandbox, three-martini business lunches for MREs (meals ready to eat) and flies. Marine recruiters report getting calls from old veterans begging to be allowed to participate. "I had an eighty-two-year-old guy call and tell me he'd whip my ass if we didn't let him back in," reported a recruiter from Ohio.

The whole thing is hard to explain, particularly the intensity of devotion Marines feel for their service. A military psychiatrist, Navy Comdr. John Cusack, says, "Time seems to stand still in the Marines. Marines don't necessarily want to fight the expected ground war, but some feel they would be robbed of glory if they didn't. The Marines are in love with the pageantry of battle, the pageantry of death."

Climate and Atmosphere

Bearing down on them all is the stunning, overwhelming heat. In the early weeks of the deployment it is the worst, even for the Marines from Twentynine Palms, California, or the soldiers from Fort Bliss, where August is never gentle. But Saudi Arabia is a different kind of heat than the soldiers have ever dealt with, a tremendous damp heat with no refuge, no escape.

And not just the heat is oppressive—Saudi Arabia is a proud, conservative nation with a very different set of values and standards from those that many arriving soldiers and marines have ever experienced. There is no beer, no women, no recreation. There is nothing to do but to try to sort some order from the chaos, clean weapons, train, write letters, wait, worry and wait some more.

The crisis comes at a curious time for the American armed forces community. For several years the all-volunteer Army, Marines, Navy and Air Force have been shrinking, a result of the demise of the Warsaw Pact as a major threat. Many career officers and senior sergeants, with many years of service, have been threatened with layoffs. There is much agitation in the press and in Congress for a peace dividend, and a much smaller, cheaper defense establishment. Both the size and content of the Army and Marine Corps are questioned, and the debate about the very existence of the Marines is raised again.

On top of all this, there is much public doubt about the quality and suitability of American weapons systems, tactics and personnel. The Abrams tank and Bradley fighting vehicle have both been criticized in the media ever since they were introduced. The Apache helicopter is widely regarded as too complicated to be reliable. The all-volunteer Army is perceived by many as a refuge for the ignorant and incompetent. Budgets for training have been shrinking for years with the result that many soldiers have little or no live-fire experience with their TOW or Dragon anti-tank missiles, M-16 rifles or machine guns. Almost none of the Army's Apache helicopter pilots have ever had a chance to actually shoot one of the Hellfire missiles they will use in wartime; at $10,000 per copy they are just too expensive to fire. And, what may be worse, almost none of the two million military personnel on active duty have ever experienced any form of combat, the veterans of Vietnam now having nearly all retired. Although the training, doctrine, personnel, aircraft and weapons systems have been tested in exercises and in small operations in Grenada and Panama, even the planners don't know for certain just what will happen if push comes to shove.

The Plan

Operation Desert Shield is based on a contingency plan, 1002-90, constructed on the possibility of a similar event. Implementing and adapting the contingency plan, though, requires a combination of political, diplomatic, and military concerns. The political and diplomatic problems come first.

First, the support and cooperation of Saudi Arabia has to be obtained—and that is neither quickly nor easily achieved. Despite the threat, many Saudi leaders worry about the effect on Saudi society of large numbers of people from alien cultures. But after a week of lobbying, Saudi Arabia consents to serve as the host nation to a proposed force.

The military response will involve two phases: the first to defend against an attack, the second to attack to retake Kuwait.

This defensive phase takes months, but by autumn enough soldiers and marines are present to prevent a major attack. Next, overwhelming combat power has to be delivered, organized, trained and equipped to fight in the desert. The entire American military establishment is quickly mobilized; active and reserve units are called up and shipped out. This phase takes six full months and taxes the resources of the Air Force, Navy, and merchant fleet. And Britain, France and many other nations agree to participate as well, sending combat divisions and support units.

AirLand Battle Doctrine

During the build-up of forces, a tactical plan is designed, based on the basic American Army doctrine called AirLand Battle. The doctrine is an adaptation of the techniques used by the Germans and Soviets in World War II, emphasizing shock, surprise, initiative and relentless attack in lightning movements. Air-Land Battle is designed to attack an enemy with such speed, violence, intensity and surprise that it is demoralized quickly and looses the will to fight.

The enemy situation the planners confront includes forty-two divisions in and around Kuwait. Iraq is well supplied and equipped with conventional and some unconventional weapons. They have excellent air force and electronic warfare assets to observe the build-up in northern Saudi Arabia. They have a lot of experience in war and have the reputation of being masters of defense. Iraq's armed forces are a tough, concentrated nut for the coalition to crack. The enemy has prepared to deal with an expected attack through Kuwait. To confront it Iraq has along the western border a corps of six divisions, two mechanized and four infantry. In the east and along the coast are five Iraqi infantry divisions. In the middle of Kuwait is a mobile reserve, with two motorized rifle divisions and three infantry divisions.

To the north, acting as theater reserve, are two tank and three infantry divisions of the Republican Guards. Together, there are two armored divisions, seven mechanized and motorized infantry and twelve conventional infantry divisions: 545,000 men, 4,200 tanks, 2,800 armored personnel carriers, 3,100 artillery tubes and 160 helicopters. In addition to conventional munitions, the force is supplied with chemical weapons and perhaps other unconventional materials.

The strategy that is designed to deal with this is not elaborate. As Gen. Colin Powell will later say, "First we're going to cut it off; then we're going to kill it."

First, they make the enemy forces expect the attack will only come up through Kuwait. All the coalition forces are concentrated across the border where Iraqi agents can see them and where Iraqi electronic warfare units can "see" their transmitters. And clearly visible just off shore are the amphibious transports of the 5th and 6th Marines expeditionary brigades, ready to storm the beaches near Kuwait city. The idea of the amphibious forces and the concentration along the border is to fix the enemy defenders in place before the battle, to make them expect and prepare for one kind of attack and then give them another.

Next, the phase called battlefield preparation. This is the work of strategic air power. The grinding process begins to remove the enemy commander's ability to see what is going on across the border when his reconnaissance aircraft can't fly, when his electronic warfare facilities are destroyed, or when observers on the ground can't send in reports by land line or radio. As roads and bridges are cut and highway travel becomes impossible, the ability of the enemy commander to move his forces becomes difficult. When supplies of fuel run low, it becomes nearly impossible. As the pressure increases, his forces

Marine LAVs on patrol near the Kuwait border. USMC

either run or hide. They become isolated, uncoordinated and begin to wither on the vine.

With the enemy's forces cut off from supplies and communications, they are ready to be killed. This could be done by the frontal assault the Iraqis expect, but that would be costly. Instead, the planners elect to shift their main effort far to the west where the defenses are light. And the allied commanders locate the enemy forces by aerial and satellite photography, electronic warfare interceptions, reports from Green Beret infiltrators and other sources. Then, the attack will go around remaining enemy formations and defeat them by seizing their support areas and devouring any resisting units in bite-sized chunks rather than whole. The process will begin with an air campaign that will start when the deadline offered by the UN on 15 January expires.

When the ground attack begins, it will be with the enemy forces isolated, blinded and reduced by the air attacks. The main effort will be 200 miles to the west, up and behind the forty-two Iraqi divisions, trapping them between the Gulf, the Euphrates River and the forces remaining along the border with Kuwait.

The Saudis, Egyptians, and Pan-Arab forces will—with the 1st and 2nd Marine Divisions and US Army's 1st Brigade of the 2nd Armored Division—retake Kuwait. The Saudis will go up the coast road, the US Marines to their left between the "elbow" and "arm pit." Another Saudi task force and a combined force of Egyptians, Syrians, and other Arab units will penetrate the border at the western limits of Kuwait's territory, about 100 miles inland.

Two corps are assembled for a long, flanking attack around Kuwait: The VII Corps will attack to the west of Wadi Al Batin across sixty miles of front; the British 1st Armoured, the American 1st Cavalry and 1st Infantry, 1st and 3rd Armored Divisions, plus the 2nd Armored Cavalry Regiment total about 100,000 soldiers. On their west flank, the XVIII Airborne Corps, including the 82nd and 101st Airborne, the 197th Infantry Brigade, and the 24th Infantry Divisions, will make the long fast sweep to the Euphrates River, trapping the enemy forces in a box.

In basic terms the plan is not complicated. The complicated part is making it happen for half a million people and all their equipment. It won't work if the supply system breaks and fuel doesn't show up when the tanks need it. It won't work if the enemy figures out what's happening and finds a way to deflect the assault. A spoiling attack by the Iraqis could do a lot of damage; so could chemical, biological or nuclear weapons, all of which the Iraqis have threatened to use.

In early December, the 197th Brigade, along with all the other players, gets its first hint of the battle plan. The brigade S-3 (plans and operations) shop sets up a planning cell. These few officers now are "read in" on the concept of the operation and the brigade's role in it. During January, only the brigade and battalion commanders are read in; not even the battalion S-3s are included at first. But the training schedule starts to provide hints; the soldiers start working on breaching techniques, clearing trenches and long road marches. Gradually other brigade players are read in, first the S-3s, then company commanders, platoon leaders and sergeants, and, by the third week in February, the soldiers know, too.

The mission for the brigade turns out to be a blocking one. They will be attached to the 24th Infantry Division and with them attack rapidly up the Euphrates River valley, blocking the Iraqi retreat or reposition. "One of the keys to the success," one battalion S-3 says, "was that the plan never changed. Our battalion issued to the company commanders *the plan*, so the entire time we were up on the border we were able to do lots of rehearsals and planning, right down at the company and platoon level. We knew exactly what we were supposed to do, cold! There wasn't any doubt in anyone's mind what was supposed to happen in their sector." One way they planned was by constructing huge sand tables with the terrain features of their sector, then rehearsing the brigade's movement in the actual attack.

By mid-February the coalition has on the ground about the same number of men and tanks as Iraq, facing across the Saudi-Kuwait border and across the beaches from the Gulf.

After concentrating these forces just where the enemy expects them, most are suddenly shifted far to the west. The move is rapid and secret, intended to deceive the Iraqis, whose ability to see the move is limited. The enemy commanders continue to expect an attack, either across the beaches or up the coast, or perhaps both, and they are ready.

As the air war begins, one kind of waiting is over for the troops on the ground. During Desert Shield there was an air of unreality about the whole thing. Many soldiers and Marines doubted that the coalition would really fight or was prepared to take the offensive and make good on its word. On 16 January, to the surprise of many, the process begins, and with a vengeance.

Chapter 2

17 January to 23 February

The Call for Fire: D-Day, 0238 Hours, 17 January

Deep in Iraq, far to the north and west of Kuwait, are two radar installations about sixty miles apart. The radars are modern, early warning systems that provide the enemy commanders information on flights above their territory. They provide a kind of "real time" view of two major corridors in the skies above the western part of the country, and that long-range view provides the Iraqi commanders crucial information for dealing with any fight. Iraqi technicians monitor their screens, watching for any hint that the coalition forces have actually begun an attack. If an attack is detected, these radars will be the long-range eyes for the guns and missile anti-aircraft defenses across the nation of Iraq, the modern and expensive systems in which Iraq has invested so heavily. But the screens are empty.

Four miles away, in the air only 20-ft. above the desert, another set of technicians watch a different set of screens on which the radar facilities themselves appear. Eight Apache helicopters, in two flights of four, have infiltrated through the dark of night. They took fire as they crossed the border, but none were lost and they slipped deeper into enemy territory. Now eight gunners study the strange, green image of the multi-function display in the center of the cockpit console. The displays show the thermal image of the antennas, buildings and vehicles and each of the helicopter gunners now identifies his assigned target,

The air war began in the early hours of 17 January when Apaches from the 1st Battalion, 101st Brigade, 101st Airborne Division, attacked two radar stations deep within Iraq. Hans Halberstadt

arms his systems and prepares to raise the curtain on the war against Iraq. They've flown almost 900 miles, much through hostile airspace, just above the desert, just under the radar's coverage, in the black of night. To one of the pilots will go the honor of firing the first shot of the war, a laser-guided Hellfire missile.

The Apaches all come from 1st Battalion, 101st Aviation Brigade, 101st Airborne Division (Air Mobile), and are part of Task Force Normandy. Each of the helicopters can carry eight Hellfire missiles, seventy-six 70-mm. rockets and 1,200 rounds of 30-mm. ammunition for the chain gun.

The Apaches are selected for this mission over other kinds of aircraft and cruise missiles for several reasons: they can penetrate without being detected, they can sustain the attack until success is complete and they carry a mix of weapons suited to the different problems of each part of the target.

The helicopters come to a hover at their battle positions, identified with precision thanks to the aircraft's inertial navigation systems. The Apache gunner sits in the forward seat, and eight gunners now search for their own special targets on the green MFD. The Fire Control panel goes from Safe to Armed. The laser designator has long since been powered up, the appropriate code entered and the gunner is almost ready for business.

The green image on the screen shows each target in clear detail, miles away. In eight helicopters, eight gunners fire laser beams at their victims, and immediately the ranges appear on the screens. At the push of a button on the control grips, each target is boxed and locked into the fire control system.

With a flash, the Hellfires leap away from the rails. The targets are painted with laser light, each missile seeking its individual code. In a series of massive explosions the radars, vans, generators and buildings are enveloped in flame, blown apart and into rubble. D-Day has begun.

The Apache strike clears the way for the rest of the allied air attack, which kicks off with a vengeance: 100 Air Force fighters pass over the Apaches as they return to Saudi Arabia. More than 100 sea-launched Tomahawk cruise missiles roar from the decks of Navy ships in the Arabian Sea and Red Sea. More than 1,000 combat aircraft sorties from carriers and airfields lift off and execute missions against targets in Iraq and Kuwait on that first day. Harriers, Hornets, Crusaders, Tomcats, Jaguars, Skyhawks and other aircraft, from many nations, begin the slow process of ripping apart the defenses of the Iraqi war machine.

The commanders call it battlefield preparation; the Iraqi defenders must have called it hell.

D-Day Across the Front

For the ground forces standing guard, there is a sudden adrenal rush about 0300 hours 17 January as the word comes down over the radio net. Sleeping officers are awakened across the front by messengers. Captain Sutherland of the 24th Infantry has his dreams interrupted by an excited messenger from the battalion Tactical Operations Center. "Sir! We've launched a hundred Tomahawk missiles! The air war's begun!" The captain thought about it for a moment, then replied, "What do you want me to do about it? Let me know when the Iraqis start getting close to our position," rolled over and went back to

The CH–47 Chinook's cavernous interior and its friendly flight crew. The CH–47 has been the Army's reliable airborne truck for 30 years. The 101st Airborne would soon rely on the Chinook's speed, range and lifting capacity during their assault deep into Iraq on G Day. Hans Halberstadt

sleep. He knows there is much to do before his unit is really ready to fight. Before going back to sleep, he has some things to think about: "It took us by surprise; we weren't ready yet. We were still down south, near a town called Al Wariah, 200 km. from our jump off positions, and had a long move to make."

The planning phase is nearly complete, and the captain has a pretty good idea of his mission. He and hundreds like him have a lot to do and a lot to worry about. Some of the units have yet to receive ammunition, vehicles, supplies, tanks or people. Supply dumps are being built to sustain the attack, if and when that happens. Rehearsals and training for specific missions need to be conducted until everyone is fully proficient with their individual roles. The prepa-

ration of the battlefield is far from incomplete. There is still much to be done.

But now the commanders, at least, have an idea when the window for the ground attack will be. That helps. And so the pace of preparation accelerates in the desert winter, while the Iraqis are worn down and the coalition forces are built up. In small ways, long before the official G Day, the war begins and the blood begins to flow.

Air War: Week One

More than 4,700 allied sorties are launched against the Iraqis that first week. The Iraqis respond with eleven Scud missiles, none aimed at the ground forces. Ten coalition aircraft go down.

An M1 Abrams in the desert. The Abrams' big turbine engine is unique among tanks. It is light, powerful, quiet, smoke free—and consumes lots of fuel and air. Clogged air filters were a frequent problem for many of *the M1 units. But the tank—subject to much criticism in the press when introduced—was a star performer. None were lost to enemy tank fire. US Army*

Marines facing Kuwait begin the ground campaign on 19 January, just two days after the air war kicks off, with artillery and combined arms raids across the border exchanging and receiving fire and casualties. On the same day elements of both XVIII and VII Corps—150,000 soldiers and all their equipment—begin the sudden, secret move west to their attack positions.

Over the next few weeks the air campaign will erode the ability of the Iraqi armed forces to talk to each other, to move people and equipment, and to get food and water to the troops. Tanks, trucks, artillery, bunkers, bridges, communications facilities and headquarters complexes are methodically destroyed, one at a time, in blossoms of fire from single, precision bomb and missile hits.

For everyone involved in the coalition planning, two basic possibilities exist for the future. One is that Iraq will quit under the pressure of the air campaign, and that a ground offensive will not be required. The other is that a ground campaign will be required to take Kuwait back.

As the air war begins no one can know how it will end, or when. It is possible that the air campaign will force a political resolution without the commitment of a risky ground campaign. It is also possible that the air campaign may be costly in lives, aircraft and commitment. In any war there are bound to be surprises.

Iraq has promised surprises in the form of weapons of mass destruction, an expression that usually means chemical, biological or nuclear weapons. Iraq has actively acquired all three types of weapons, and

An air defense system rattles forward. The missiles are all heat-seekers, similar to ones used by fighter aircraft.
USMC

the delivery systems required for each, so the threat is not an empty one. As the battle begins millions wait and worry about what the response from Iraq will be. And none worry more than the soldiers and Marines on the ground, facing the defenses of a strange, well-equipped, huge army only a few miles away.

Air War: Week Two

In the air war, 15,300 sorties are flown against the Iraqis during the second week. They respond with forty-three Scuds. Seven coalition aircraft are lost. The 1st Cavalry Division begins combat operations, part of the deception campaign. On the ground, there are skirmishes and raids along the border.

Deep within Iraq, the secret warriors are attacking in subtle ways everywhere. In the enemy capital, Baghdad, British SAS (Special Air Service) and SBS (Special Boat Service) soldiers disguised as Iraqis set up laser designators to direct GBU-15 bombs to precision hits on special targets. Other special forces soldiers wander the country disguised as businessmen, vendors and Bedouin tribesmen. They collect information, plant homing beacons and neutralize key enemy officers. SAS teams driving special dune-buggy vehicles mounting .50-cal. and 7.62-mm. machine guns prowl the western desert looking for Scud launchers and downed pilots. They have a SAT-COM radio, night-vision goggles and perhaps more courage than discretion.

From perfectly camouflaged holes in the desert, overlooking critical terrain, special forces recon teams watch for movement. All that pokes above the surface is a small periscope. Similar holes hide snipers with the immense .50-cal. Haskins rifle. These target interdiction teams are trained to be invisible, to move undetected, to observe and report, and to kill with the first shot at ranges of more than a kilometer.

Air War: Week Three

Air forces fly 17,000 sorties. Six Scuds are launched. About ninety enemy aircraft fly to Iran, and nobody knows why. Iraq is taking a pounding.

The western border of Kuwait is a little valley, the Wadi Al Batin. At its southern end, down in Saudi Arabia, is the town of Hafir Al Batin. The wadi is a dry riverbed, a natural terrain feature that makes military commanders say to themselves, "What a great place for an attack!"

So in late winter, the 1st Cav arrives with tanks, Bradleys, tents, trucks and a lot of people and sets up shop along the border looking up into the little valley. At first, the Cav defends Hafir Al Batin from an attack down the wadi. Then, they begin to make the Iraqis worry about an attack going the other way.

Deception Plan

There are three major deception missions in the Kuwait theater of operations as the days count down toward the one called G. The first is the Marine amphibious force off shore, threatening all of Kuwait's coastline. That pins about eight enemy division in place to fight them if and when they come ashore. Since they're facing the Gulf, they can't help anywhere else. That takes them out of the battle.

Another deception is the massing of forces across the southern border with Kuwait. It is an obvious route for an attack. The Iraqis defend it heavily, build it up and prepare to take the hit from that direction. Their forces are once more locked into position, physically and mentally. More divisions are under the remote control of the coalition planners.

A third deception mission is tasked to the 1st Cavalry Division. They're the westernmost unit during the final months of the build-up, and they have two major missions in the grand plan. One will be to function as a reserve once the battle begins after G Day. But until then, the Cav has to convince the Iraqi commanders that they'll be leading the charge up the Wadi Al Batin along the western border of Kuwait.

As the air war rages, Pan-Arab infantry train in Saudi Arabia. USMC

They'll fix more Iraqi resources where they can't hurt anybody. It starts with a screening mission, Bradleys and Cobras teamed up, aggressively patrolling the border during the last few days of January and beginning of February but with few shots fired.

On 13 February, 1st Cavalry Division turns up the heat with a series of feints, demonstrations and raids. MLRS batteries roll up to the border at the wadi and launch their multi-purpose arrows at command and control sites identified by air. Every day after 13 February the Iraqis are hit one way or another: tube artillery and Multiple-Launch Rocket System (MLRS) rockets shoot at them. The 2nd Brigade sends breaching teams to the berm with armored combat earthmovers (ACE) and conduct breaches. The Iraqis can't tell if it's the real thing or a rehearsal. Lanes are blown in the berm while artillery falls on the defenders beyond, TOW missiles destroy bunkers and thin armor, and tank main guns fire into any Iraqi target that is presented. The Cav crosses through, explores the neighborhood, and under cover of night, pulls back. But they leave inflatable "tanks" and noisemakers to simulate a force remaining on the position. They also leave a few brave scouts dug into shallow holes in the desert to report on the enemy reaction.

The scouts are the division's long-range recon teams. Using binoculars and night-vision goggles, they wait until the Iraqi troops move in to investigate, then

Iraqi soldiers had planted extensive minefields along the Kuwaiti border, so US Army engineers practiced techniques for clearing paths through the minefields. Bravo Company, 27th Engineer Battalion, trains, using the MICLIC, or Mine-Clearing Line Charge, just before G Day. Kirby Lee Vaughn

call artillery down on the enemy. The Iraqis try to begin an aggressive mine-laying program, but they are ambushed by the Cav every night.

The Cav's Apaches and Cobras raid up the wadi, too. After an artillery prep SEAD (suppression of enemy air defenses) mission, the helicopters slip up the little valley and shoot up any bunkers, vehicles or troop concentrations they find.

G Minus 3

On 19 February the 1st Cav's 2nd Brigade gets tasked with one of the early invasions of Iraq, a reconnaissance-in-force directly up the wadi. The brigade's mission is to see if there's a weak spot where the Cav can get through, but to do it without getting itself shot up in the process.

Although the Cav has been tapped to be the reserve force for VII Corps, that doesn't stop them from planning offensive operations, and 2nd Brigade's staff has eleven plans on the shelf for contingencies. This recon is one, and they turn it into an operations order. The 2nd Brigade kicks off up the wadi on the next day, 20 February. In the lead is Task Force 1/5 Cav: two companies of tanks, two of Bradleys, a TOW company, a company of engineers, plus an air defense unit and some support from other units.

At about 1300 the scouts bump into a small force of enemy infantry that starts shooting at them from bunkers. The scouts engage, then peel off to let the big guns up to clear the position. They take prisoners and while handing them off to units in the rear, come under fire from anti-tank guns well emplaced on the reverse slope of a little ridge. The whole task force comes under intense direct and indirect fire from AT-12 guns and mortars. The brigade commander's track is an M113 with lots of antennas—an obvious target if you're an Iraqi. Several high-velocity rounds rip over the head of the commander, Col. Randolph House, before he gets the vehicle moved to safer ground. Nearby, one of the Vulcans providing air defense isn't so lucky; it takes a direct hit, decapitating the track commander. The Alpha Company, 1/5 Cav executive officer's Bradley starts to shoot up the enemy position, but takes a hit in the turret, and its gunner is instantly killed the same way. Another Bradley is hit in the turret, launching the two TOW missiles. An Abrams tank runs over a huge anti-armor mine; the blast engulfs the tank in smoke and dirt shoots 150 ft. into the air.

The Bradleys hose the enemy position with 25-mm. and 7.62-mm. coax, and the tanks quickly move on line and engage with main and .50-cal. guns. One of the Bradley gunners in the lead sees enemy soldiers run into a bunker about 1,500 meters away; he pops a couple of 25-mm. high-explosive rounds into the aperture. The soldiers run out, and the gunner hoses them with the coaxial machine gun. He spots another group of five dive into another bunker, and he sends them a few 25-mm. HE rounds, too. Out they come, down they go. It happens to him again, twice. In a few minutes the Iraqis across the entire complex are either bleeding, running or hiding.

The Bradleys, though damaged, are still driveable, and head to the rear. And, after a few hours' effort, the tank damaged by mines also drives away.

The wounded crew men are extracted, but while moving them mortar rounds start dropping on the rescuers. PFC Ardon Cooper, Alpha Company, 1/5 Cav shields one of the wounded crew and takes a full load of shrapnel himself. He's med-evaced out, but the damage is too great. He dies later that night not knowing he'll receive the Silver Star for his gallantry.

The recon continues, and discovers the hard way that more than a hundred artillery tubes have been infiltrated and concealed in the wadi. The Iraqis pull off the camouflage nets and put the tubes to work. Unfortunately for the enemy gun crews, though, the guns now become excellent targets for the Air Force A-10s orbiting overhead, and for the rest of the day, the Cav's recon mission becomes one of playing turkey at a turkey shoot. The enemy artillery becomes targets

POW compounds were built in the desert to accommodate prisoners to be captured during the forthcoming ground campaign. USMC

themselves, and every A-10 in the theater concentrates on them for the rest of the day. That night the task force pulls back to the berm.

Khafji: 29-31 January

On the evening of 29 January, all along the Saudi-Kuwait border, are eight little border observation posts (OPs), nerve endings for the commanders to the rear. These OPs are manned by Saudis, Army Green Berets, Navy SEALs (Sea-Air-Land commandos), Force Recon marines, and even Delta Force soldiers. OP-8 is on the coast road, manned by SEALs and other special ops people. In the distance, they hear the roar of engines and the squeal of tank tracks approaching. After a few minutes, tank columns can be seen, gun tubes to the rear. The teams are uncertain of the motives of the tanks, suspecting a mass surrender. But the turrets swing around and the guns begin to fire. So much for the surrender idea. The Saudis beat a hasty retreat, sound the alarm and try to get off a few quick shots. The little outposts are quickly overrun, the Iraqi force blasts by down the coast highway toward the town of Khafji to the south.

The little Saudi community called Khafji was once a prosperous city, catering primarily to the oil industry personnel who work the hundreds of rigs in the area. But with the threat of invasion from Iraq's massed forces just up the road, the town's residents abandon shops, hotels, homes and businesses. It is an eerie, silent ghost town, neglected even by the marines and Arab forces who patrol the area, although a special operations center occupies one of the buildings.

An Iraqi tank destroyed near Khafji. The fighting for Khafji was fierce, but allied forces decimated the Iraqi attackers. USMC

The attack on Khafji is one part of a larger scheme involving four battalions of tanks from the Iraqi 5th Mechanized Division, Soviet-built T-55s and T-62s. They attack in three violent probes and break across a front of fifty miles of border, from Umm Hujul on the west to Khafji on the east.

At the same time Khafji is taken, special operations teams far to the west identify other tank forces moving south, out of Kuwait in the vicinity of the "elbow." These teams, too, are quickly overrun, some managing to escape, others going to ground to hide out for a while. Their radios still work, though, and air support and artillery are called and begin to engage. Iraqi electronic warfare (EW) units succeed in jamming all the marines' radios, except for a new system called SINGARS (Single-Channel Ground and Airborne Radio System) designed to cope with EW activities. The task force commander, Lt. Col. Clifford Myers, is able to report his predicament with the SINGARS system, and help is on the way.

At about 2200, a company of American marines from the 1st Light Armored Infantry Battalion, part of Task Force Shepherd, confronts the force attempting a breakout. Their lightly armored vehicles and cannon are not supposed to be a match for true tanks, but they use them against the Iraqi armor anyway and destroy twenty-two Iraqi armored vehicles.

One of the prisoners they take is the commander of the Iraqi force. He tells his captors that, during the battle, he ordered a subordinate unit to come up and provide support but instead they ran to the north.

It is the first major fight of the war. Twelve marines die in the encounter, some from friendly fire. They are the first Americans to die in the ground war.

Once the Saudis have retreated, the Iraqi forces quickly begin to explore the city, looting anything of value along the way. Personnel from the special operations center put their escape and evade training at the SERE (Survive, Evade, Resist, Escape) school to good work and tippytoe as quickly to the south as they can.

The speed and surprise of the attack catches two small Marine recon teams in the town, cut off and isolated from friendly forces except by radio. One is led by Corporal Ingraham. They quickly establish an escape and evasion plan that they hope will prevent them from becoming prisoners.

Evading enemy patrols, they make their way to the Hilton hotel, and dash to the top of the building where they crank up their faithful radio and start calling the military equivalent of 911. With the Iraqis strolling around under the window, the marines manage to contact 1st Battalion, 3rd Marine Regi-ment, an artillery unit that is fortunately in range of both the radio and the 155-mm. howitzers owned and operated by the unit.

While the recon teams are keeping busy staying alive, other marines and Saudis set up a blocking position five kilometers to the south. There, on the afternoon of 30 January, Marine, Saudi, and Army officers spread their maps on the hood of a Humvee (HMMWV—the hi-tech replacement for the Jeep) and plan the counterattack.

The 25-mm. armor-piercing rounds for the chain gun are prepared by two Marine LAV crewmen. One also is draped with belts of 7.62-mm. rounds for the pedestal-mounted M60s. The 25-mm. gun won't kill a tank, but it will get the crew's attention and make them button up. The 25-mm. is designed for light armor (personnel carriers, trucks) and bunkers; it hits accurately to over a mile. USMC

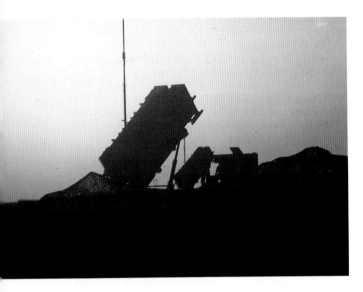

A Patriot missile system awaits incoming Scuds in Saudi Arabia. The effectiveness of the Patriot was questioned before it began knocking Scuds out of the sky. US Army

A fallen Scud lies where it fell in the Saudi desert. Members of the 101st Airborne inscribe it with a soldierly thought or two. Later, it was carted away for closer inspection. US Army/Sp. Elliot

For the Saudi commander, Colonel Turkey, there are several motivations. One is that the fighting ability of the Arab forces is in doubt. Another is that his nation has been invaded and occupied. Another is that the Marine recon teams trapped in the city are part of Task Force Taro and Marines and Saudis have become brothers in arms, particularly deserving of rescue.

The Arab force is ready to attack, but assaults like this need artillery preparation. The prep is delayed when the Marine battery objects to a fire mission without observation, and an argument with the battery delays the counterattack.

Finally, the Saudi commander says, "I have orders to attack, and I *will* attack in ten minutes. With or without the artillery prep!" The battery fires the prep mission. At 2200 hours, the Arab forces, a combination of tanks and APCs from Saudi, Qatar, and other Gulf nations, pile into their vehicles and attack north.

The Arab plan isn't fancy—it's more of a cavalry charge. They go up there knowing that they are probably going to lose their lives. They go anyway.

For two days the little Marine band plays cat and mouse with the enemy soldiers, some of whom enter the building. Although the marines have rigged the stairwell with claymore mines, any direct confrontation with the invaders is likely to end badly for the squad. So while awaiting rescue, the marines keep busy by calling in artillery and air strikes on the enemy. At one point, the corporal explains that the reason he's whispering is that enemy soldiers are on the floor directly below.

But the young marine's skill as an artillery spotter is thoroughly tested. In the street below, an armored personnel carrier stops with a load of troops. They begin to pile out and prepare to start a house-to-house search. The marines call for fire, even though the target is perilously close; a round lands directly on the armored personnel carrier, splitting it in half and killing or wounding all the twenty enemy soldiers nearby.

Although the Saudis pull out of the town, they don't go far, and they're *mad!* With them is a Marine captain, an adviser to the King Abdul Aziz Brigade (Task Force Abu Bakar), and an ANGLICO team to coordinate gunfire. The Saudis immediately begin planning a counterattack to retake Khafji, but encounter a problem with a Marine artillery battery. Without an observer to report on impacts, the battery isn't supposed to fire, and they refuse to shoot a prep for the Saudi counterattack. But they won't let the counterattack go without a prep, and rounds drop on the Iraqis, even without an observer to spot them.

The Arab forces' attack isn't elegant, sophisticated, or polished. They simply assault the place head on, with speed and violence, killing and being killed. The Iraqi forces are hunted down. Those that don't surrender quickly are killed quickly. The marines are still trapped, though, and the capture of the town and rescue mission takes time.

While the Arabs engage Iraqi units on the outskirts, the Marines call for help again. This time it is not one, but seventeen personnel carriers in the street below. Far to the rear the battery fires a volley and the huge shells destroy all the vehicles in a moment.

Secondary explosions from large stores of ammunition on the carriers add to the destruction. The dazed Iraqi survivors attempt to escape, and the recon team shifts the battery's fire and calls for another volley. There are now few left to escape.

For two days the recon team moves from one deserted building to another. And for those same two days, Qatari and Saudi armor units in the area work at taking the town back. The final counterattack comes at night, and the operation order for the Arab units is simple: attack Khafji to rescue US Marines trapped there. With the help of coalition air power, they fight the Iraqi tankers on the outskirts, then inside the town. The Arab units lose nineteen killed

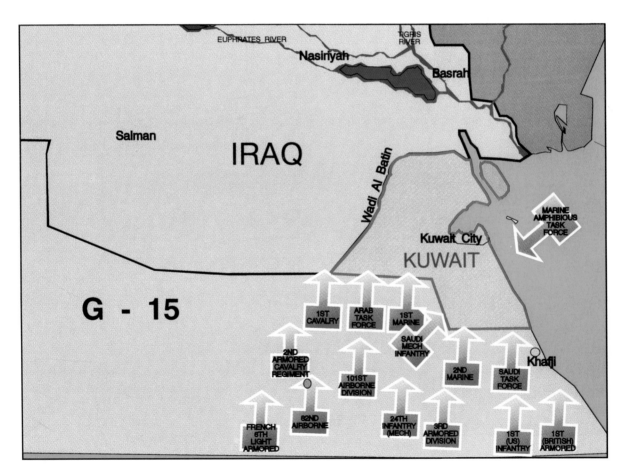

Fifteen days before the ground war began, allied troops clustered on the Saudi-Kuwaiti border, seemingly poised to strike into Kuwait.

and thirty-six wounded before the Iraqis are defeated. At last the recon team is recovered; none has been killed, only one wounded by shrapnel.

The attack costs the Iraqis thirty-three tanks and twenty-eight personnel carriers and an unknown number of soldiers killed and wounded in Khafji. At least ten enemy tanks are destroyed in the attack at Al Wafra to the west at a cost of three armored personnel carriers. Air power in the form of Marine Cobra attack helicopters, Air Force AC-130 Spectre gunships, plus fighters of several different kinds destroy more of the force during its incursion and retreat. The masses of enemy targets are just what the pilots have been hoping for. It is, as one says, "like flipping on the light in the kitchen at night and the cockroaches start scurrying."

There are some lessons in the Iraqi offensive for the attackers and defenders. For one thing, it demonstrates an Iraqi interest in the spoiling attack. It shows, also, that they are poorly coordinated, equipped and trained. It is the first test of both American and Arab battle skills. It proves that the Arab units will attack, take casualties and still drive on. It tests coalition weapons, tactics, communications, air-

power, and individuals. The Iraqis lose; the coalition wins. There are lessons learned on both sides. Captain Molofsky, the Marine liasion officer, sums it up this way:

"The battle for Khafji had a dramatic effect on the development of the scheme of maneuver for the entire allied campaign. It solidified in the minds of a number of people that the Saudis would be partners in this attack. Prior to Khafji there were serious questions about the ability or enthusiasm for a fight on the part of the Pan-Arab forces. Khafji proved, without question, that the Saudis were committed, brave, willing. It proved that they would, with the slimmest of orders, put their lives on the line to protect the kingdom. That was Marines and Arabs standing shoulder to shoulder. When the Saudi commander heard there were Marines trapped in the town he said to me, 'We attack! We attack!'

"Khafji was significant, too, because it was the only time the outcome was ever in question. When the Iraqis attacked south across the border, for a couple of days nobody knew if they were as tough as their reputation, if they were going to continue their attack south, or if we could stand up to them. Once that battle was over, all those questions were answered.

"The Saudis lost nineteen dead and thirty-six wounded—some triple amputees. It was a hell of a battle. The Iraqis fought. The situation was confusing and the outcome in question."

Another Marine sums it up differently; looking at the destruction of the Iraqi force he digs his camera out of a flack jacket pocket and observes, "This here is a Kodak moment!"

Skirmishes and Scouts

After Khafji things gradually warm up all across the Kuwait–Saudi Arabia border. It starts with artillery raids and small scouting reconnaissances, the heat gradually applied against the enemy across the border. Marine gunners duel with enemy artillery across the border in Kuwait. The big 155-mm. howitzers reach six miles into enemy territory, and beyond, seeking out targets and destroying them.

The 24th Infantry Division has been training south of the Kuwait border, one of the many divisions concentrated near where the Iraqis believe the assault will come. Then, the time comes for the move. A week before the scheduled offensive, a few days after D-Day, the 24th moves out, down the pipeline road, to an assembly position west of the Neutral Zone.

Now everybody is read in on the plan: attack across the border up to the town of Al Busayyah and a

French Foreign Legion soldiers demonstrate some of their weapons to the men of Bravo Company, 27th Engineer Battalion. Bravo Company was attached to a French unit during the first days of the ground campaign. Kirby Lee Vaughn

crucial road junction to block enemy forces trying to escape from the Seventh Corps attack on the right. It is supposed to take several days, minimum, and may be a hard fight. As a contingency, the 24th may be tasked with taking Jalibah airfield, far to the north and near the Euphrates River. After that, perhaps into Basra or Kuwait. That was the plan, and it was—according to the planners—going to take awhile.

By this time everybody has a pretty good idea of when the ground assault will officially kick off. And they also know that they aren't going to wait that long to apply the heat to the opposing team.

Although the Iraqis are not supposed to know an attack will occur in the 24th's new sector, the division begins aggressive scout patrols. At G Minus 5, a reinforced company of tanks and Bradleys from 3/15 Inf is ordered up to the berm to take out an enemy observation post that overlooks a piece of key terrain. One platoon sets up on the berm itself and a reinforced squad moves up into a little protective gully and across toward the enemy position. An artillery FIST team makes the call for fire, and uses a laser designator to mark the target for a Copperhead projectile fired from far in the rear. The observation post disappears, the victim of a single round.

The final days and nights are busy ones for the scouts. They creep across the border, exploring the routes the battalions will use, checking for minefields, fortifications, troop concentrations and enemy recon elements.

At about G Minus 7, Captain Rennebaum, his anti-tank company and his 82nd Airborne company, D/1/325 Parachute Infantry Regiment, are flown out to the little border town of Rafha, dumped in the desert, and pointed at the border. The division's primary anti-tank weapon on the ground are the TOW missiles, mounted on Humvees. The missiles have thermal sight sensors that permit the gunners to study enemy activity at ranges of several miles and engage targets at about two miles on the darkest night, through rain or fog. So the TOWs get put right up front. The anti-tank platoons really got a workout.

As one 82nd soldier remembered: "We assumed responsibility from six kilometers back, to the border. We established three ambushes and observation points on high terrain where we could watch the whole valley. All night long they'd be observing through the TOW night sight. They picked up a lot. At night the Iraqis would do a little probing, trying to identify our positions."

But as the days and weeks of the initial phase of Desert Storm unfold, the soldiers and Marines, the British and Saudi tankers, the Kuwaiti and Egyptian

infantry, and all the other forces of all the other nations watch and rehearse and wonder. They are often cold, usually dirty, sometimes hungry, and occasionally scared. Nearly all are untested by combat, and they wonder how they'll do.

Army Sp. Clarence Cash dies on New Year's Eve when his tank is hit by a rocket-propelled grenade. L. Cpl. David Snyder, a Marine, is killed on a patrol early in February, weeks before G Day.

It is obvious to everyone on the ground facing the border that the days now trickle down to a precious few. The tension and anxiety gradually escalate, and people find different ways to cope with the waiting. Many find comfort from their religious training and beliefs, although the services in the field are sometimes a little unorthodox.

The chaplain attached to the 1st Battalion of the 3rd Marines finished hearing confession from an unusually large number of Marines, then assigned a penance of ten Our Father's and ten Hail Mary's. One of the Marines piped up, "How do they go, Father?"

"You should have learned that in Catholic school!" the priest responded.

"What Catholic school, Father? I'm Baptist!"

Over in the 4th Marine sector, two recon teams are sent deep into enemy territory on G Minus 2; their

An M1 Abrams sits in the dubious shade of camouflage netting, waiting to hit the trail in the days before G Day. USMC

41

A French Legionnaire poses in front of his Renault squad vehicle. Kirby Lee Vaughn

mission is to find routes through the mines and obstacles for Task Force Grizzly. The first team, from 2/7, is discovered after sixteen hours, and mortar rounds and artillery starts falling on them. But the fire is not accurate, so the team carries on with the mission. Both recon teams work up to within two miles of the first belt of trenches and minefields, about ten miles in from the border.

M1 and M1A1 Abrams Main Battle Tanks

The M1 and M1A1 Abrams main battle tanks saw their first combat in the Operation Desert Storm. After many years of criticism of the tank's engine, gun, sights and other systems, the design has been vindicated in its trial by fire. It was slammed for being too heavy (126,000 pounds), too expensive ($3.5 million each) and too unreliable. It uses a crew of four: driver, loader, gunner and commander. They and their tank are part of a platoon, usually four tanks, working as a team.

The great virtues of the Abrams are its speed and its gun system. It is powered by a 1,500 hp gas turbine engine, like that used in airplanes, that consumes lots of fuel but delivers tremendous power in a small, light package. The tank is supposed to be limited to about 45 mph, but crews say they moved much faster during the race toward Basra. Each Abrams carries about 500 gallons of fuel, enough for about 200 miles of travel in a tactical environment.

The tank's main gun is a 120-mm. smoothbore cannon, which is stabilized and computer corrected. The stabilization system keeps the gun on target no matter how much the tank is bouncing around or where it is maneuvering. The gun is aimed with the assistance of a computer that measures wind speed, air density and temperature, barrel warpage, and type of ammunition; a laser range-finder provides extremely accurate information about the distance to the target.

Either the tank commander (usually a sergeant) or the gunner can engage targets. In battle, both scan constantly for enemy threats, and are alert to radio calls from other units in the task force who may have spotted the enemy. Once a target is identified, the commander calls "Target!" to alert the crew that he wants to fire, then, "Tank, front, 1,800 meters," to identify it and make sure the gunner sees it too. Using his override control, the commander aims the gun at the same time he calls for the kind of ammunition he wants to use against the target. He tracks the center of the target with a special grip that looks like something out of a fighter airplane. One button fires a laser at the target, computing the range and entering the data as part of the fire control solution. "Sabot!" is his call, and the loader, jammed into the turret on the left, extracts one from the rack, flips it end for end, slides it into the breach, which slams shut. "Up!" the loader calls, meaning the gun is loaded and ready to fire. "On the way!" tells the crew (especially the loader) to stay clear of the recoil, then he fires.

Inside, the sound of the huge gun isn't very loud, and the recoil isn't heavy. The tank rocks a bit. The sight is obscured for a moment by the hot gasses, then the target is visible again as the projectile slams into center of mass. Hundreds of Iraqi T-72s, T-55s, and T-62s were destroyed this way, sometimes exploding immediately, other times catching fire gradually, "brewing up" into an inferno as the ammunition and fuel begins to burn. Often, turrets were blown far into the air, landing many meters from flaming hulls.

Tank targets get serviced with a long, heavy, steel dart only about an inch in diameter. But it leaves the gun traveling about a mile a second; its tremendous kinetic energy actually melts a hole in the side of the target, spraying the inside with molten metal. Lightly armored vehicles, buildings, and bunkers get HEAT rounds, high explosive projectiles that blow up on contact. Both are tracers so you actually watch the projectile zip across the battlefield with amazing speed.

The Abrams' armor is a composite of steel alloy, ceramics, and depleted uranium that protects the crew from most anti-tank threats. None were destroyed by enemy tank fire in the war. On one occasion a disabled Abrams was supposed to be destroyed by its own unit when it couldn't be recovered. The unit commander fired a sabot round at the tank and it bounced off.

The M1A1 is deadly out to over a mile, with first-shot kills routine to about 1¼ miles. The Iraqis' T-72, by contrast, is accurate to only about 1,000 meters and lacks the stabilized sight system and the thermal imaging system. If the Abrams can stay out of the T-72's effective engagement range, it's "point, game, match" to the M1A1 every time.

One of the Marines, S. Sgt. Charles Restifo, a combat engineer, boldly prowls around an enemy minefield with such confidence that the Iraqi defenders—an entire company—surrender to him. While the enemy soldiers surrender, other Iraqi units begin shelling everybody. But even so, the enemy prisoners of war (EPWs) help clear a lane through the mines and into captivity for themselves and their captors.

The same day, out to the west, the 24th Infantry sends scouts from 1/15 deep into Iraq to check the battalion's route and to play cat and mouse with Iraqi patrols in the area. Their cross-border recon produces red flares shooting up into the night, brief firefights at long range, then silence as the Iraqi soldiers withdraw deeper into their territory. The scouts peer through their PVS-5 night-vision goggles and see trucks and troops scurrying around in the distance, eight miles in from the border. A missile is observed as it is launched from a site even deeper, the location carefully marked for further attention. Then they retreat back to the berm.

All along the Saudi-Kuwait border, coalition armored forces are now poised at their line of departure. British Chieftain tanks from the famous Desert Rats, French Foreign Legionnaires, Saudis, Egyptians, Kuwaitis and the rest are now all formed up on line, across hundreds of miles of desert. Gun tubes, missile launchers and machine guns all point north. Through night-vision goggles, thermal sights and binoculars, thousands of soldiers and marines from dozens of nations watch and wait for midnight.

Iraqi troops torched hundreds of oil wells in Kuwait, filling the air with thick, oily smoke. USAF/T. Sgt. Heimer

Even before the assault begins, Kuwait has been invaded. Forward, invisible combat engineers are clearing lanes for the assault, searching methodically for anti-tank and anti-personnel mines. As they move through the obstacles they trail a 2-in. ribbon of engineer tape to mark the boundaries of the lane. It is one of the most hazardous jobs in any army.

While the air campaign pecks at the enemy another phase of the plan is at work. Although the Iraqis quickly lose their airborne "eyes," there are still plenty of enemy scouts watching the activity of the coalition forces across the border, and part of the plan is designed expressly for them. This part involves a massive deception campaign, intended to make the enemy commanders believe that the attack—when it comes—will make its major thrust directly up into

Marine LAVs stare across the border into Kuwait. The inside is crowded enough already, so the baggage gets stowed outside. USMC

National Training Center

Virtually all the soldiers and marines interviewed for this book have praised the intensity and realism of the training they received before the war, crediting it for saving lives and getting the job done quickly and efficiently. For the Army's soldiers, the best training was probably conducted at the National Training Center (NTC), a thousand square mile expanse of desert in Southern California. It is a stark, hot, empty stretch of desert where temperatures often exceed 120 deg. F. in summer, where the wind blows cold in winter, and where the instructors fight the students for two long weeks. Virtually every Army armor unit that deployed to Desert Storm fought at NTC—and lost.

The idea behind the training is to give a brigade-size unit a chance to go up against the best Soviet-style motorized rifle regiment in the world, the kind of equipment, organization, and doctrine that Iraq (and many other nations) use. "Wars" at NTC don't stop for weekends, holidays or anything else. Visiting units have to drive out into the desert and deal with an opponent much like the Iraqis might have been, had the Iraqis fought.

A Soviet-built BTLB armored personnel carrier of the type used by Iraq. This one, however, is owned by the US Army and is used to train American armored units to deal with Soviet-style weapons and tactics at the National Training Center. NTC was one of the reasons for the success of American armored forces in war; most fought harder battles there than in the Gulf.

During the build-up and planning phases of Desert Storm and Desert Shield, the Army used NTC to test ways of dealing with Iraqi defenses. During the fall, a huge anti-tank ditch was constructed on the floor of the desert, duplicating one built by the Iraqis in Kuwait. American armor units experimented with breaching techniques on the obstacle while the NTC enemy defended with artillery simulators and tear gas.

The NTC experience was shorter than the Gulf deployment, but many of the soldiers who fought at both places will say that NTC was more difficult. The lessons learned certainly saved lives. One battalion commander recalled getting caught at NTC by a spoiling attack by the "enemy," and when he went to fight for real, he made sure he was always ready to deal with a counterattack.

The dust-choked conditions of the NTC training grounds near Fort Irwin, California, were nearly identical to those experienced by American tankers in Iraq. Hans Halberstadt

Kuwait. Most of the allied divisions are concentrated along the border, the vast desert to the west left mostly empty during the weeks of the air campaign.

Up front are the Saudi task force, the 101st and 82nd Airborne Divisions, the 24th Mechanized and the 3rd Armored Cavalry. And just off shore is a large Marine landing force, the 4th and 5th Brigades, threatening the beaches near Kuwait City. The intention is to fix the defenders in place, to force them to defend against massed armor and amphibious forces aimed at Kuwait.

For many, it is like a play or a dream unfolding—hard to really believe that there will be a real attack against a real enemy who will fire back real bullets.

Scouts from all the forward deployed units patrol the border area, often exploring across it. As the time for the big assault nears, the scouts' work intensifies. They begin identifying routes through the berms and minefields, calling in artillery on targets and spying on the loyal opposition.

The US Marines have a number of armored vehicles that are unique to their branch of service, and one of these is the large, wheeled armored recon vehicle officially called a LAV (Light Armored Vehicle), but unofficially named many things, some not printable. The light armored vehicles are faster than tanks, able to zoom around the desert at 50 mph or better—a desirable feature when you're being shot at. And in late February, the Marines are doing a lot of raiding.

The raids are part deception, part recon. For the Marines in *Fat Chick*, one of the 2nd Light Armored Infantry Battalion's armored vehicles, it was also part scary. Their mission in the days before the ground campaign kicks off is to locate gaps in the defenses, draw artillery fire, counter recon and deception.

Midmorning on 21 February, *Fat Chick*, in company with three platoons of other LAVs from Charlie Company, shoots its way into Kuwait with its 25-mm. Bushmaster chain gun. The group explores enemy territory, moving deeper at a rapid rate and at first with little opposition.

The squadron makes it about five miles into Iraq to a ridge and a power line. Apparently they've deceived the Iraqis entirely too well, convincing the enemy that the invasion is on and that the main effort is *Fat Chick* and her buddies. The Iraqis shoot back, not with the little stuff, but with large-bore artillery and 122-mm. rockets—lots of them. Moving deeper into enemy territory produces more and more artillery. Sagger anti-tank missiles whiz by.

At about 1300 *Fat Chick* and her friends all make a break for the exit, run home and yell for help. The help comes from the 5th Battalion, 10th Marine Regiment, firing artillery in support. Charlie Company and *Fat Chick* head back to Kuwait and Power Line Ridge. Enemy tanks are dug in across the desert to their front, so Charlie Company makes the call for fire and soon artillery from 5/10 starts landing on the tanks.

Deeper in Kuwait, *Fat Chick* and the other vehicles start taking mortar rounds. One lands on a Humvee, destroying it in dramatic fashion. Although the vehicle is completely unarmored, the crew emerges from the wreckage, unhurt. Two Iraqi trucks appear on a road nearby. Both explode when 25-mm. high-explosive rounds hit their cargoes of fuel and ammunition.

Enemy tanks appear, counterattacking. Close air support takes care of them, but the artillery and anti-tank fire intensifies. Two FROG missiles land on one of the platoon's positions—with no damage done.

22 February, G Minus 2

Around daylight, G Minus 2, Charlie Company encounters enemy tanks, T-62s, firing at them. While *Fat Chick* and some of the other LAVs fire their Bushmasters, the TOW vehicles move in to shoot. The first TOW is a dud, the second goes wild, the third hits. The tank explodes in half. One of the gunners, L. Cpl. Frank Steiner IV, kills two tanks. Back in the States, newspapers report minor artillery skirmishes along the border.

For another two days, Charlie prowls out front, heavily engaged; Lance Corporal Steiner gets two more tanks. They withdraw back to Saudi Arabia about midnight. At 0400 they will attack with 6th Marine Regiment when the real invasion begins.

With variations, the same thing is going on all across the entire 300-mile front. Scouts from the 82nd Airborne, the 24th Infantry and the 101st Airborne far to the west, and the Marines, the Pan-Arab and the Saudi task forces looking into Kuwait, all creep forward into the defenses of the enemy. Not many soldiers and marines are involved, but enough to help deceive the enemy forces, to keep them wondering what is really happening.

23 February, G Minus 1

The Arab units will breach the heaviest defenses, the best prepared, most obvious routes. To prepare, they assemble a task force with every kind of heavy equipment they can find. Commercial bulldozers are modified with improvised armor, painted and aimed at the border. A Green Beret captain helps them plan and coordinate. On the night before the assault, the breaching task force stretches for miles across the northern Saudi Arabian desert. Beside the vehicles, over open fires, the Arab soldiers cook their goat meat and wonder about the morning.

Virtually all the units probe the defenses they'll have to cross, identifying possible routes through the minefields, enemy artillery positions, outposts, fortifications and troop concentrations. And some units actually move across the border long before the official G Day, occupying positions near the obstacle belt and waiting for the big attack to begin. Over between the Elbow and the Armpit two Marine task forces from 1st Marine Division are already in position at the belt, providing security for the armor task forces that will soon come blasting through. As one marine remembered: "About 1100 we were pushing everybody forward, because by this time the enemy recon elements had pulled back. We occupied our positions, not a shot fired. We were the first guys across the border."

Lt. Col. Ray Cole, 1st Marine Division operations officer: "What we tried early on—with deception and with the raids—was to make his front line forces, and even his commanders, uncertain about exactly where we were going to come. Then, when we did attack, it was in strength on a narrow front to get forces behind his two principal lines of defense behind the obstacle barriers—make the defenders irrelevant to the battle. And that's exactly what took place.

"By G-Day we have two regiments north of the first obstacle belt, holding the flank. Papa Bear, and Ripper have moved to their attack positions four kilometers from their point of breach inside Kuwait. Task Force X-Ray, our anti-armor force, is still outside Kuwait with its helicopters.

"We commence to breach about 0630."

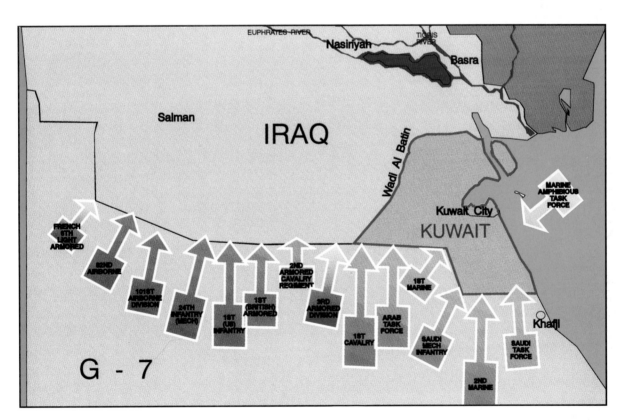

By seven days before the ground war began, allied forces had quietly moved westward in preparation for their flanking attack into Iraq.

Chapter 3

24 February: G Day

Midnight, 23-24 February

For the quarter of a million soldiers and marines waiting for their individual units to move, the early hours of 23 February seem an eternity. Some expect to attack at 0400. Others aren't supposed to cross the line of departure (LD) until the next day.

For a few, the war has already begun, and they've been fighting for days—regardless of the official time for the assault. But most are trying to sleep somewhere, sitting in personnel carriers or sprawled uncomfortably in tank turrets or in the back of trucks. But even at midnight, many are still awake: standing guard, refueling vehicles, bringing up supplies, finalizing plans or just worrying.

The early minutes of 24 February finds four Arab and three American divisions poised on the edge of Kuwait, ready to attack. Most already have elements across, screening and securing the first few miles of enemy territory. On this night, as for many nights during weeks past, scouts from Iraqi units spar with scouts from British, Saudi, French, Syrian and American units: a few tracers in the gloom, the crump of a mortar round, dim figures moving somewhere off in the distance.

Offshore, two Marine brigades afloat threatened an amphibious landing along the Gulf coast. After an epic road march, nine American divisions along with one French and one British teamed up in two massive corps, the VII and XVIII, and have moved to attack positions far to the west. From here they will attempt

Moving up, a Marine LAV heads for the berm and into enemy territory. USMC

a massive flanking maneuver intended to trap the Iraqi forces against the Euphrates River marshes.

The French 6th Light Armored Division has traveled farthest, nearly 300 miles out Pipeline Road to the little town of Rafah. Their mission will be to attack north, secure the left flank of the battlefield, and screen against any Iraqi threats that might come from the west. Their objective is the airfield at Salman.

Next to them is the American 82nd Airborne. The division has been flown in on C-130s. They'll be attached to the French for the first part of the attack, then peel off and drive on toward the Euphrates. The 82nd has the least armor of any of the divisions participating.

Attacking up through the center is XVIII Corps, composed of the 101st Airborne, the 24th Infantry and the 3rd Armored Cavalry Regiment. The 101st was a heroic paratroop division in World War II, but now is master of the helicopter-borne air assault mission. The 101st's mission on the first day is a big one: the largest air assault in history. They'll fly deep into Iraq to establish a support base for the corps.

On the ground, the 24th Infantry, with the 197th Infantry Brigade attached, will form the right flank for XVIII corps. Together, they'll drive all the way to the Euphrates River, then turn right to chase the Republican Guards all the way to Basra.

VII Corps forms the center of the attackers and according to the plan will comprise the main effort. It includes the American 1st and 3rd Armored Divisions, 2nd Armored Cavalry Regiment, 1st Infantry and 1st Cavalry Divisions, plus the famous British 1st Armored Division. The VII Corps mission is to sweep up into Iraq and hit the hard-core Republican Guards mobile reserve in the center of Kuwait.

The actual liberation of Kuwait gets tasked to Arab units, with US Marine support. A division including Egyptian and Syrian units and three Saudi task forces will attack across the heaviest defensive positions, focusing their effort on Kuwait City.

Flanking the Arab attack are the 1st and 2nd Marine Divisions, together known now as the 1st Marine Expeditionary Force; they're reinforced by the US Army's 1st Brigade, 2nd Armored Division. They are organized into task forces: two will be infantry, Grizzly and Taro, and they'll walk into Kuwait; two will be tanks and mechanized infantry, Ripper and Papa Bear; one light armored infantry, Shepherd; and one artillery, King. The initial mission for the 1st Marine Expeditionary Force is to get behind the enemy forces facing the obstacles and to move up to the airfield at Al Jaber, Kuwait, and the Burqan oil field.

The Marine attack actually begins on the night of 23 February. Grizzly and Taro move across the border, into the first obstacles, securing them for Ripper and Papa Bear, the armor assault to follow on G Day.

Most of these forces are heavily armored. The infantry soldiers and marines will ride to battle in personnel carriers or trucks, protected by accom-

A CH-47 shows up in the green multi-function screen of an OH-58 Delta model. The display is linked to a "million dollar beach ball" above the rotor and these thermal viewing systems and designators make the OH-58 the best scout/spotter in the world. The night vision and thermal imaging systems on allied tanks, airplanes and helicopters gave them a real advantage over their Iraqi opponents. Hans Halberstadt

panying tanks. Thousands of vehicles are strung out across the desert, waiting for the order for their units to move. For some, the order is due in the early hours of the morning. For others, it won't come until the next day. For a few, the order has been executed already and they are already deep inside enemy territory.

0400, G Day: The Attack Begins

At 0400 the Marines' 1st and 2nd divisions, already deep in Kuwait, attack across the berm, into the obstacles, through the minefields. There are two belts with a space of several hundred meters in between. The first belt in Task Force Papa Bear's sector is set up oddly: the mines are sitting on the ground, easily visible. And fences mark the leading and trailing edges.

Papa Bear gets past the first belt unopposed and starts the breach on the second where the mines are buried, using line charges and mine plow tanks. Artillery and mortar fire, machine gun and tank guns engage the breaching teams. One tank's plow catches a mine and the tank is disabled; the crew eject, uninjured, but the lane is blocked. Another tank loses a plow, blocking a lane. Instead of four routes, Papa Bear goes through on one.

S. Sgt. Daniel Kur clears lanes through minefields by hand, picking up the mines and carrying them away from the breach. A combat dozer arrives to help carve a path through the defenses, but hits a mine, knocking the sergeant flat. He recovers, collects the shaken driver, and keeps the advance moving forward. Then, under fire from enemy rockets and small arms, he directs two infantry battalions, one artillery battalion and the regimental headquarters, through the breach.

Elsewhere, Sgt. Brian Zickafoose, a sniper with a Marine Badger vehicle moves far forward on a route reconnaissance. He spots an observation post and mortar battery, and they spot him. They start dropping high-explosive rounds on his position. He lights them up with a hand-held laser designator while close air support aircraft make strikes on the enemy positions. Both enemy positions are destroyed.

Sgt. Gordon Gregory, also breaching the minefields, leads a recon platoon forward, looking for a path through the obstacle belt. The enemy soldiers spot the platoon and start dropping mortar and artillery fire on them while shooting at the team with machine guns and AKs. The sergeant runs to collect the scattered members of the team, making himself a conspicuous target for the Iraqi gunners. Two members of the unit remain deep in the minefield. The sergeant works his way to them while shrapnel zips past his head.

The obstacle belt is a busy place on G Day. At the same time, Cpl. Michael Kilpatrick, another member of 3/9, comes under intense artillery fire. Since his job is to drive the fire support and recon vehicle, he gets to work and calls in air strikes on artillery. The enemy gunners drop mortar and artillery rounds nearby, splattering the vehicle with shrapnel and making phone conversation difficult. But soon the airplanes are overhead, attacking the artillery and silencing the batteries. Col. Ray Cole: "By 1030 we have eleven lanes through the obstacle belt and we're moving through. Ripper is through, Papa Bear is through. Ripper starts taking artillery."

The task forces are engaged by small enemy units, tanks and infantry, which fire on the attackers. They are fired on in return, but the Marine advance doesn't stop to deal with them. Instead, they are brushed aside. Anything in front of the attackers, though, is destroyed by the massive application of combat power. Colonel Cole: "Our approach was to refuse to give battle to the flanks, a vicious attack head-on to get behind these forces as well. We found that once we decisively killed the ones in front of us, got behind them, it either routed them in panic, or caused them to give up."

A French Puma helicopter skims the ground behind advancing American troops. Kirby Lee Vaughn

Artillery is rained on the task forces, but it is quickly turned off with counter-battery artillery fire missions or close air support each time. On forty-two occasions during G Day, the marines use their TPQ-36 Firefinder radar to spot incoming artillery rounds and identify the location of their battery. Air support is called in on the guns, and they are eliminated before having a chance to fire a second round.

The Al Burqan oilfield burns nearby, hundreds of wells thundering fire. The sky to the east is a black wall of smoke. The sound of the fires pervades everything, even battle, with a kind of rumbling roar. As one soldier said, "It was a kind of continuous drum-beat, times six or seven hundred, as the oil rushes out of the ground and immediately catches fire. You almost can't hear anything else. A huge black cloud of smoke, guns firing, artillery firing—it was kind of eerie. The assistant division commander turns to me and says, 'This has got to be like Dante's Inferno.'"

At 0800 the 101st Airborne launches an immense air assault, sixty miles into Iraq to establish a forward operating base (FOB) called Cobra. 1st Battalion of the 502nd Infantry assaults by Black Hawk helicopters to secure the northwest corner of the objective, runs into a battalion of enemy, and quickly defeats them. The 3rd Battalion of the 327th Infantry fights a reinforced platoon of Iraqis guarding a huge cache of weapons and ammunition. Close air support arrives, hosing down the complex with rockets, cannon and machine gun fire. Then loudspeaker-carrying aircraft appear, advising the Iraqi soldiers to surrender—and they quit.

Fifty CH-47 Chinook helicopters carry huge fuel bladders, pumps, hoses and related equipment to a spot west of the Iraqi town of Salman. They set up eighteen rapid refuel sites to support the advance. In three hours the gas stations are open for business.

Cobra quickly grows to massive size, twenty miles by forty miles, larger than the 101st's home base, Fort Campbell, Kentucky. Cobra permits the division's Black Hawk helicopters to fly from bases in Saudi Arabia all the way into the Euphrates River valley, refuel at Cobra on the way back, and return for another load. Apaches and Cobras start dropping in for fuel and ammunition for their hunting trips. With the FOB established, the 101st is now capable—if anyone wants—of launching air assault troop lifts into Baghdad itself.

At 1300 the 24th Infantry kicks off, fifteen hours sooner than expected, leading the charge to the Euphrates River.

About the same time, the Saudis and Pan-Arab divisions attack into Kuwait on the marines' right flank. Six lanes are cut into the obstacles, and the Arab liberation of Kuwait begins. Columns of vehicles—M60 tanks of American manufacture, French-built Mark F3 tanks, Cadillac-Gage V-150 personnel carriers, old American M119 personnel carriers, British Land Rovers, French Milan weapons carriers, Soviet built BMPs—miles long wait to cross. The flags of many nations fly from antennas, the uniforms are of amazing variety. It is a colorful pageant that moves up the coast, past Khafji, and at the enemy. The Arab breaching teams cut six lanes through the minefields. Artillery falls ineffectively on the lead elements, but isn't adjusted, and they are through.

The Big Red One

Lt. Col. Dave Marlin leads 3rd Battalion, 37th Armored Brigade, the 1st Infantry Division ("The Big Red One") as part of the VII Corps assault: "I had the tank battalion that came through after the initial breach. You'd have to say that the 'pucker factor' was sky high, because everybody understood that once across the berm you were going at the enemy. At that point we had a very high expectation that they'd use chemical weapons. I came across with fifty-eight tanks.... Anything that moved, died. That was their only choice, surrender or die. Once you cleared the breach, anything was a target."

The Big Red One attacks on line, with two brigades forward and one back, up to the berm. Two miles from the trench line the tank gunners can see through the thermal sights that the defenses are manned by hundreds of enemy soldiers preparing a reception. At a range of four miles, enemy tanks can be seen moving about behind the trench line. Several tanks fire high-explosive rounds into the trench complex, and several hundred of the enemy quickly surrender. Others stand their ground, however, and are engaged.

Sixteen lanes are cleared by plow-equipped tanks; they comb the ground of mines, leading the force through, then are tasked with clearing the trenches. The division boils through in their tracks, then begins to engage targets to the front. Anything that comes up "hot" in the thermal sight is killed. Some of the Iraqis want to fight, and engage the American tanks with any weapon available: tank main guns, mortars, small arms, rockets or anti-aircraft artillery.

The ones that chose to fight die quickly. The plow tanks simply fill in the trench, burying some of the enemy alive while others peck at the armor with machine gun bullets. The Iraqis are completely outclassed and it is over in an hour.

The big operation requires perfect coordination and performance from eighteen division-sized elements, stretching across hundreds of miles of front. At midnight on 24 February, the initial phase of the attack has already begun in hundreds of places, across hundreds of miles. So the scout mission is particularly important now, to make sure the task forces can actually move across the minefields and trenches.

Radios crackle in the night: TOW missile gunners, scanning the battlefield across the berm, positively identify six howitzers moving far forward. Are they friendly or hostile? The gunners are ready to fire. Regiment calls Division, and tensions are higher than ever—then the unit that had positively identified the howitzers calls back to report that the objects were now positively identified as camels.

197th Brigade: Into Iraq

"Everybody knew exactly what they were going to do, how they were going to do it, and how they related to each other, and it really paid off," a company commander says. But not every detail comes off exactly as planned: the 197th Brigade was supposed to cross its line of departure twenty-four-hours after the 101st and the other units to the west had begun their attack. "We were just starting to move into our attack positions," the company commander says, "when we got the word—the morning of the 24th—that we were going today! A lot of detailed planning on how to move in and how to get across the berm were thrown out the window, and it turned into a rodeo. It really went fast from that point forward!" The actual execute order comes down at 0900, and three hours later the brigade is across the berm, into Iraq.

The company commander remembered that "Our first thought was that the other units had run into trouble. We kept hearing 'Execute, execute, execute!' coming down on the radio, and we thought we were going to have to go bail them out. We all thought that the 101st, 82nd and the French had run into something they couldn't handle." There had been a lot of talk also about an Iraqi spoiling attack, and as the attack began many in the brigade expected immediate contact. And that wasn't the only worry for the brigade: "The 101st was far to our left, and we were the left flank for the brigade, which meant that there was a big gap between us and the nearest friendly unit. Our left flank was always open, and we thought it was just a matter of time until we got attacked from over there."

But as they rolled across the desert, through a terrific sand storm, there is no contact, no attack, for

eighty-six miles deep into enemy territory. Visibility at times is only 15 ft.—later it will be worse. The sandstorm has several effects: one is to eliminate part of

Advancing American tanks found plenty of targets for their main guns. These crewmen restock their tank with sabot rounds. USMC

55

the detailed planning the S–3 (operations) section has done to determine the exact route for the task force's advance. Instead, a straight line is drawn to the refuel point and everybody drives for it. For the soldiers in the tracks, there is a certain amount of anxiety, but for many it is moderated by the knowledge that the long wait is finally over. Far out in front are the brigades' scouts, screening the force and leading through the ragged terrain. Above and in front of the scouts are the brigades' faithful little air force, the Apache and Cobra helicopters.

One soldier remembered the drive: "Dark, raining like mad, out in the middle of nowhere, we ran into an enormous wadi—can't go anywhere because it's fifty feet straight down, scouts can't find a way around it, so we went *into* it. We dug fifty feet down into it with our 'dozers and got the whole formation through. Unbelievable! And that wadi was going in the right direction, took us where we wanted to go.

"I was really amazed at the American soldier's ability to take a situation, figure it out quickly, and do something about it, get the job done.

"I never had the feeling that it wouldn't work. We had practiced it so often, gone through numerous exercises, everybody knew what they were doing. I knew exactly where everybody was thanks to our

Private First Class Dozier, a 2nd Cav recon scout, rides atop his Humvee. US Army

global positioning systems. I never felt that we wouldn't pull it off, but I just didn't want to have a lot of casualties doing it.

"I didn't know initially what we were going to run into. I guess the key to our success was the indirect approach that we used. We went where they weren't. We got into the enemy rear and flank, his defenses were oriented the other way. The Air Force played a big role. The close air support was great; we used it twice."

Task Force Ripper

The 7th Marines, now part of Task Force Ripper, are—along with the 82nd Airborne—the veterans of the campaign. They've been here since the scary, scorching days of August. Now, in the damp chill of desert winter they're tired of waiting and poised to finally attack. The rehearsal has brought them right up to their line of departure for the real performance. For the First Battalion the G Day mission will be to attack north, breach two defensive belts of mines, ditches and bunkers, then attack enemy forces at the Kuwaiti Emir's farm complex, clear the farm and dominate it by fire; from there, swing around to the northwest and attack Al Jaber airfield from the northeast. On order, continue north and seize Kuwait International Airport.

The 7th Marines organized their forces in a classic way, a mixture of armor and infantry called cross-attaching. "Take a company of infantry and give that to the tanks; the tank battalion takes the infantry and gives a company of tanks in return. That's how you make a tank-infantry team," one of the platoon leaders explains. "We had CAAT [antitank] teams forward, followed by Team TANK—two platoons of tanks and one of mech infantry, plus their engineers—followed by the command group and the 'jump CP' followed by Team MECH—Bravo Company, 1st Battalion, 7th Marines with one platoon of tanks and two platoons of infantry. Charlie Company provided the reserve, followed by all our combat trains"— the support vehicles with fuel, ammunition, supplies and the rest.

"I was with one of the CAT teams up on the right flank, at the forward edge of the battalion," one lieutenant remembered. "The engineers had been making cuts in the sand berm that marked the border for several days, and there must have been at least a dozen of them. Ours were marked with blue chemlights." The marines drive along the berm, looking for their assigned lanes, then turn and cross into enemy territory. Drivers announce the event to the passengers of the big Amtracks (amphibious tracked vehicles) and other battlefield busses; instead of excitement, in many of the vehicles, the marines start to relax. Some go to sleep. The long wait is over.

Off to the northwest an airstrike is visible to the crews who have a view outside, but none of the famous Iraqi artillery, small arms fire, flaming trenches or other hazards everybody had worried about. Land mines are everywhere, but sitting on the surface of the desert, rather than hidden. Most are easily avoided, although one M 60 discovers one the hard way, loosing a track in the process. No one is hurt, and the crew climbs down from the tank.

The first obstacle belt is breached, then the excitement begins. "We started taking incoming 82-mm. mortar fire," the platoon leader says, "and I'm in thin-skinned vehicles. So this is what it's going to be like from here on in! I started hearing med-evac calls on my radio and we started worrying. The vehicles started taking hits from the shrapnel, and pieces started falling off—but nobody got hurt!" The Iraqi mortar fire drops in the same place, without the adjustment any competent mortar team would apply. So the marines just drive around the impact areas.

The two obstacle belts are easily breached, and then the task force rolls on, forty miles deep into Kuwait, with only scattered enemy contact. At first light a few prisoners are taken. One, an Iraqi captain fluent in English, tells the marines that the famous, battle-hardened enemy is just waiting for a chance to surrender. Most don't believe him.

At about 1300 the 7th Marines' first objective for G Day is reached: the Emir's farm. Around the same

Private First Class Jimmerson, Bravo Company, 5th Engineers, lends a hand to the 24th Infantry Division. The track is an M-9 ACE (Armored Combat Earth- *mover), the prime system for breaching the Iraqi berms.* US Army

time, Task Force Shepherd, moves to the east to screen. They begin taking fire from enemy tanks as they come through the breach, but none of the force is destroyed. Ahead, the oil field fires roar, the sky is solid black and the air is dense with grease. One of the company commanders from Shepherd about to enter the Burqan oil field, keys his microphone and announces to his compadres, "Welcome to the gates of hell!"

As his force begins to penetrate the smoke, enemy tanks materialize only 300 meters away. They are invisible until their guns flash. There is a sudden,

A French Gazelle helicopter skims the ground as equipment and troops push north into Iraq. Kirby Lee Vaughn

fierce gunfight that begins with the LAVs firing their 25-mm. Bushmasters at the tanks. The 25-mm. rounds are able to scratch the paint on a main battle tank, but not much more. What they accomplish, though, is to distract the enemy gunners, shoot off a few aerials, and break some of the vision blocks required to aim the guns. So while the LAVs are busy annoying the tanks, the TOW vehicles hastily maneuver to firing positions and let go. All of the tanks are killed, and the little force rumbles deeper into the gloom of the Burqan.

With part of his flock guarding the flanks from the oil field, the commander of Task Force Shepherd moves the rest northward, toward the day's objective, the airfield at Al Jaber. Four miles north of the field they link up with Ripper to their west and prepare to bed down for the night. Visibility is 100 meters, more or less. Prisoners tell them to expect a counterattack.

The Grizzly, Ripper, Taro, Shepherd and Papa Bear task forces move on to the day's objective, Al Jaber airfield. At about 1700 the Marines secure their positions and break open the meals ready to eat (MREs) while artillery falls around their positions.

G Day 24 February finds the 1st Cav still with its reserve mission. Reserves don't go to war unless things get either very *bad* or very *good*. As the day progresses, things start looking good, and 2nd Brigade gets a warning order: prepare to move; attack up the middle of Wadi Al Batin to make sure the forces are already there, stay there. The brigade moves that night in a huge wedge formation eight miles across and seven deep, 1/5 Cav in the lead. During the night they engage two tanks and a ZSU-23-4 heavy anti-aircraft system with Copperhead laser-guided artillery projectiles: three targets, three rounds, three hits on center-of-mass.

G Day starts quietly for the 24th Mech and their compadres, the 197th Inf Brigade. According to the plan, they won't be going anywhere until the morning of the second day. Third Battalion, 15th Infantry will take the lead for the division when the assault crosses into enemy territory. The commander is Lt. Col. Raymond Barrett: "I had the lead battalion, in the lead brigade, in the lead division for the major push up into the Euphrates River Valley. We were out on the pointy end of the stick. I fought the battle out of my Bradley, forward, just behind the lead company. It was hellacious!"

For Lieutenant Colonel Barrett and the rest of 3rd Battalion—as well as the entire 24th Division— the stress level this morning is low. The ground attack may be going full steam elsewhere, but the 24th isn't supposed to kick off until tomorrow, day two. The morning of G Day is low-key, enlivened only by a promotion ceremony. And a radio message about noon. The message gets everybody scurrying into action: "Saddle up! We're out of here at 1500 today!"

Lieutenant Colonel Barrett: "We started the battle fifteen hours sooner than we expected, with two hours notice. Fortunately, I had pushed a heavy company forward the night before, scouts, tanks, mech infantry, about ten kilometers into Iraq. So I had already secured the line of departure. The other companies had moved up to a preattack position, so we were postured to move. Except for all the logistics [fuel, food, water] which we were scheduled to start receiving about 1200. About 1300 I was ordered to be across the LD [line of departure] at 1500. That caused us a little problem. But it was a matter of 'Okay, guys, it's moved up. Let's crank!' A change in mindset."

The Bradleys and tanks and trucks all need to be fueled, a million tasks that were going to get done during the afternoon and evening now get done, or forgotten, at a run. Many of the soldiers have been up all night rehearsing and had planned to get some sleep before the attack, but sleep will have to wait. The old chemical warfare suits are quickly discarded in favor of fresh ones. Everyone wonders if they'll be needed and if they will work. In one company both the

A mine clearing rake on an M-728 Combat Engineer vehicle from the 24th Infantry Division clears a trail through an Iraqi minefield. US Army

commander's and the executive officer's vehicles choose this moment to break and a mad scurry ensues to fix them and also to find replacements.

Lieutenant Colonel Barrett: "We crossed at 1500 hours in a driving windstorm, nine hundred men in two tank companies, mortars, scouts, command and control, air defense assets, an engineer company of one hundred and fifty men, and a hundred and sixty or so vehicles kicking up a tremendous amount of dust. So trying to control the combat formations of the vehicles as we moved quickly across this terrain so I didn't have a company get lost somewhere, or create a gap, a vulnerability in the formation—we had to work extremely hard, talking back and forth. I was worried about the tanks ingesting dust as I was ingesting dust! It was very hard to command and control.

"We had prepared for this for six months, and it was high stress, high anxiety. It was great! The scouts were out forward, and they found the routes up the escarpments. Using our global positioning systems we knew where we were all the time, continued to move

all night long, refueled in the middle of the night two thirds of the way to the first objective. At daybreak we were close to our objective, ninety kilometers deep into Iraq. We got on to the objective, consolidated, and refueled, then moved on again.

"It was a very difficult move, done extremely well. No vehicles dropped out. Nobody broke down on a 170 kilometer move, and we maintained 100% of our combat power."

But they move out on time, the first vehicles edging across into dangerous territory about 1530. Like the Marines, and all the other forces, the vehicles search for the cleared lanes through the obstacles and are quickly past the much-feared Iraqi defenses.

The weather has been bad and now gets worse. Rain mixes with blowing sand kicked up by the vehicles and is driven against the task force by a relentless wind. The result is what one of the soldiers calls a mudstorm. Visibility is zero at times, and often only a few feet. Even so, the formation of tanks and other vehicles lumbers across the ragged, desperate landscape.

Colonel Zanini, commander of the 3rd Brigade, 1st (US) Armored Division, briefs the troops before a mission. US Army

A few miles into Iraq they encounter terrain that is impassable even for tracked vehicles. A cliff confronts the task force, its face much steeper than indicated on the maps. On top, intelligence reports say, may be an enemy force. But the lead elements probe forward, the scouts search to left and right for alternatives, and in the end an entire brigade is forced onto a little road. In column, tremendously vulnerable, they drive into the Iraqi night, up and over the terrain. It was an immense traffic jam in the middle of the desert. But they made it up to the top without opposition, any enemy forces that may have been present now gone.

"It was the worst weather you can imagine," a young sergeant says, "but it was perfect for us. Our thermal sights could see out to 1,500 meters, so we could see where we were going. But otherwise you couldn't see a thing! It was perfect weather for an attack!"

Captain Rennebaum of the 82nd Airborne: "The MLRS were moving with us, and firing right over our heads! They'd stop, and it was wham-wham-wham. It was beautiful! Like nothing we'd ever trained for—all the safety requirements, all that crap, out the window! When the MLRS stopped and the launchers went up, everybody just moved to the side. That was the highlight of Day One. Everybody was firing, and it was awesome."

Captain Rennebaum's Delta Company gets a call from Brigade about 2000. The anti-armor company will be leading the attack on the next objective, a large complex on a high hill. The attack is initially supposed to be from the flank.

Captain Rennebaum remembered: "The battalion commander said, 'You and your five platoons are going to lead the attack.' Of course, you get tight in the stomach, but you don't have time to think about it because there's so much to be done. I'm sure the platoons felt the same way, but it was happening so fast I don't think anybody had time to think. Then we get to about 8 kilometers from the objective, and we get a FRAGO [fragmentary order] that says we aren't going to take them from the flank, we [are] going to make a frontal attack. Holy sh--! I'm going to be up front—what am I doing up here? I'm not supposed to be here! So I have to tell the platoons. And they're calling back, saying 'Are you *sure* . . . ?'

"I tell them 'We're going to take them from the front. There should be an artillery prep on the target. We'll stop at about 2500 meters. As soon as you identify targets, go ahead and engage. It's a battalion-sized objective, we're not sure the size of the enemy force, they're dug in, there are bunkers up there.' So we

continue to move. About 4000 meters out, we start taking mortar fire. They're shooting at us from about 2000 meters to our front. The commander says, 'Continue to move forward.' It wasn't like they had to bracket us because we moved right in to them."

It is fully dark. The enemy gunners start dropping 105-mm. howitzer rounds and mortars on Delta Company's vehicles, now only a thousand meters or so from the enemy positions. Delta presses on, but now the TOW gunners start finding targets in their sights, and call back for permission to fire. The commander calls brigade for permission, and immediately hears "Engage!" They fire on a truck on the high ground and immediately call back "Hit!" Then the platoons identify bunkers, call for permission to shoot again. This time the company commander doesn't bother with brigade; "Engage!," he says.

They fire five TOW missiles into the bunkers, blowing each apart in sudden, violent fireballs before one of the vehicles calls back, "I see white flags and people coming out of the bunkers!"

Captain Rennebaum: "It was like kicking over an ant nest. There were people swarming everywhere. I called 'Cease fire!' and we started moving up toward the objective. I'd never seen anything like these men, hundreds of them! We could have waxed all of them. To end this thing without any real bloodshed, I felt good about that—at the same time I felt sad for these guys."

Up on the objective, a senior officer is captured. He tells them that only the howitzer crew wants to fight, and tells the Delta Company commander that they don't have to shoot anymore. In the bunkers are lots of weapons, equipment and ammunition, all new and in excellent condition—but no food or water for the soldiers. Some diehard Iraqi shoots an RPG at one of the vehicles, but it goes over the hood, surprising the crew but doing no other harm. The gunner isn't found.

Combat engineers get busy blowing up bunkers and supplies, weapons and vehicles. The dust and smoke they add to the air mixes with the dust from all the attacking vehicles, making visibility in places limited.

From some places on the high ground, the whole pageant of the assault is spread out below. The main supply route (MSR) can be seen, bumper to bumper with trucks loaded with fuel, ammunition, supplies, engineer equipment and logistics support units of all types, trailing back toward Saudi Arabia.

Captain Rennebaum: "That thing was jammed! You could not move a vehicle through there, bumper to bumper both ways. Supplies coming up, enemy prisoners going to the rear—total chaos.

"That was my one day up there, being a hero. It was a thrill, something I'll never forget, an experience I wish everybody could go through. Everything went exactly as we practiced it, as we planned it. We didn't lose anybody! I went up to the battalion commander and told him, 'Sh--, sir, that was fun!'"

Sitrep, G Day

G Day hasn't been fun for everyone. As the first full day of ground combat concludes, XVIII and VII

AirLand Battle

The strategies and tactics used against the Iraqis were based on the Army's basic warfighting doctrine, called AirLand Battle. The basic idea of AirLand Battle is to win with minimum cost. The concepts in the doctrine aren't new or original; it is based on tactics used by both the Germans and Soviets during World War II, along with the lessons learned from wars hundreds and thousands of years in the past. The concept uses infantry, artillery, armor, attack helicopters and Air Force ground attack planes in a coordinated, unified force called the combined arms team.

AirLand Battle is based on the idea that winning comes from the efforts of many people working in harmony toward a single goal. Even the lowest soldier is expected to understand the commander's intent. By understanding the goal, soldiers are able to improvise and adapt within the chaos of battle. In Operation Desert Storm even the most junior infantry soldier had an understanding of the whole grand scheme.

Initiative: It involves taking initiative, going on the offensive and applying massive combat power in a way that surprises the enemy and puts him on the defensive. Coalition forces took the initiative by shifting the main effort from the Kuwait border, far to the west, then attacking rapidly through terrain thought impassable by the Iraqis. Even junior leaders or individual soldiers are taught to take the initiative when appropriate if there is a chance to help achieve the commander's intent.

The speed, power and surprise of the attack by XVIII and VII corps not only demoralized the enemy units in its path, but throughout the enemy force. They were galvanized into inaction by an attack that was far larger, far more violent, and far away from what they expected.

Agility: In AirLand Battle, attacks are large, rapid, movements of overwhelming intensity; helicopters, tanks, mobile artillery and trucks provide agility. The 101st Airborne's assault into the depths of Iraqi territory on the first day of the ground campaign was an excellent example of strategic agility on a grand scale. The supply base they established permitted further activity on a large front, all the way to the Euphrates River. Within hours of the beginning of the ground war, coalition tanks were only 150 miles from the enemy capital.

Depth: This doctrine encourages commanders to mass their combat power and support so that the attack can be sustained in an overwhelming, relentless assault. This depth prevents the enemy from recovering, reacting, or resting. An essential, unheralded part of the strategy involves the part of the force that keeps the fighting units supplied with food, fuel, ammunition and repair facilities to sustain the momentum of the attack. Several times during the campaign, units found themselves almost out of gas just before a scheduled attack, only to have supporting fuel tankers show up in the middle of nowhere, in the middle of the night. The supply officers and truck drivers who refueled the tanks added depth to the battle, which contributed to its speed and success.

Synchronization: The attacks are synchronized for maximum effect. Artillery, armor, infantry, all are coordinated to shock the enemy and destroy his will to resist. The Iraqi forces were besieged from all sides, from the air and the ground, from tanks, attack helicopters, guns and rockets. The efforts of half a million people were coordinated through a system of communications and a basic plan. The battle ended up being accelerated, but it stayed synchronized: divisions moved together, protecting each other's vulnerable flanks. The two huge armored corps sliced up and across Iraq at high speed, in low visibility, and still maintained formation. Artillery prep fires were dropped on targets just before assaults, then lifted just as the tanks and personnel carriers moved onto the objective, another kind of synchronization that saves lives.

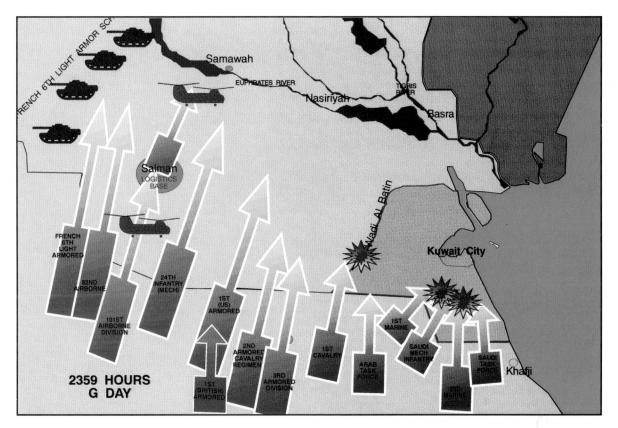

At midnight on the first official day of the ground campaign, Iraq's forces have already been isolated, caught in a trap built from the French 7th Light Armored Division—which has sealed off the western edge of the battlefield—the Euphrates River, the massed forces of the coalition, and the waters of the Gulf. The western forces—XVIII and VII corps—race north, then pivot east while heavy fighting inside Kuwait rapidly destroys the Iraqi forces.

Corps are deep into Iraq, far ahead of their schedules. The 101st is hauling fuel and supplies into the logistics base east of Salman. Midnight finds tanks, personnel carriers, Humvees and trucks pushing across the desert, pausing to refuel but not to rest. For the commanders there are two worries: will the attack run out of fuel? And will the attack run into real resistance?

Marine and Arab units aren't resting either. They're through the major obstacle belts and minefields, driving on toward Kuwait City against stiffening resistance. The 1st Marines, by evening, have taken Al Jaber airfield; they're halfway to Kuwait City.

To the rear, the unsung heroes of the campaign drive on. They're the young privates, men and women, driving the big 5-ton trucks that keep the attack going. Back in the rear, too, are the field hospitals waiting for the dead and wounded. As the first day ends, the corpsmen, doctors, nurses and operating room personnel are amazed at the few coalition casualties. Enemy action has killed four and wounded twenty-one allied soldiers and marines across the entire front on G Day.

Ten thousand enemy soldiers surrendered on G Day, a flood which is more of a problem for the attacking forces than the occasional scattered resistance they encounter. The enemy soldiers, amazingly, often treat the coalition forces as liberators. This is not the reception Saddam Hussein promised, but only day one is over, not the war.

The attack continues.

Chapter 4

25 February: G Plus 1

Midnight, twenty-four hours into the war, finds Lieutenant Colonel Barrett and his task force on the top of a mesa, 100 miles into Iraq. XVIII Airborne Corps is blasting ahead to the Euphrates River, shoving aside or rolling over enemy resistance. The French 6th Light Armored has taken its objective, Salman airfield, and has set up its screen to the west, securing the battlefield from unwelcome visitors.

Now the 82nd Airborne peels off from the French and rejoins its XVIII Airborne Corps partners, the 101st Airborne and the 24th Infantry. Together, they blast toward their objectives, airfields and critical highways to the north. The terrain for all of them has been vile. Inside the lurching, noisy, cold vehicles the young soldiers wait for the order to dismount, assault the enemy—and perhaps die. Many try to sleep; some do.

At the same time, to the east, I Marine Expeditionary Force is in positions north of Al Jaber airfield and the Burqan oil complex. The marines from Twentynine Palms, who've waited the longest, are now part of the 1st Marine Division. They're fighting alongside Saudi and Pan-Arab divisions, and twenty-four hours into the war they are about forty kilometers into the heaviest defensive positions the Iraqis have built. Midnight for the marines doesn't look a lot different from midday, the smoke from hundreds of burning oil wells making the sky opaque.

Around midnight, Task Force Shepherd's commander, Lieutenant Colonel Myers, gets tasked to provide a guard for the division command post (CP).

A UH-60 Black Hawk, mainstay of the 101st Airborne's air assault mission. The Black Hawk is strong enough to carry anything you can fit aboard. Hans Halberstadt

He chops Bravo Company TOW platoon and the company commander for the job, Capt. Ed Ray. The captain objects to the rear echelon assignment. He's been missing all the action and complains that at the rate things are going he will miss out on the whole war. But he leads his troop of good scouts off into the gloom, twenty kilometers to the rear.

Midnight also finds the 4th and 5th Marine expeditionary brigades still aboard their ships in the Persian Gulf, all keyed up with no place to go.

For all of them, the first day had brought some surprises: The equipment has worked, for the most part, better than anyone expected. The plan worked well, too; the advance is incredibly fast, the opposition light. The soldiers and marines, from old sergeants and colonels to baby-faced eighteen-year-old privates, are getting an odd sort of confidence from the experience. It is still tempered with caution, though, and many wonder how long it will be until the war really begins.

While the XVIII and VII Corps have been off for their ride in the country, the Marine and Arab divisions have been fighting hard and moving slowly. For task forces Ripper, Papa Bear, Grizzly and Shepherd, the distance hasn't been so terribly far, but the marines have had to fight hard nearly all the way. Seventy-two hours into the campaign, the 1st and 2nd Marine Divisions have—in company with the Arab forces—surrounded Kuwait City. The liberation of the capital city will be the honor of the Kuwaitis themselves, with other Arab contingents providing support. But first, there is the airport to secure.

Counterattack!

About midnight, 1st Marine Division starts getting reports that a large enemy armor concentration is in the burning oil field. The first comes from an enemy POW who indicates that a counterattack is supposed to begin soon. A document is captured indicating the same thing. At 0400, an intel source provides grid locations for two enemy armor brigades preparing to conduct the counterattack. As one marine remembered: "We had more pieces to the puzzle than we wanted. By that time we had four battalions of artillery in position to provide fire support. We directed all four to fire a 'time-on-target' mission. We adjusted a thousand meters to the east, and they did it again. Then all kinds of enemy action started breaking loose."

At the Burqan oil field, the 1st Marines encounter dug-in enemy soldiers. The Iraqis fire on the marines and seem ready to make a stand. The marines call for fire from their supporting artillery. The fire mission is a time-on-target barrage that is timed so that every shell explodes over the target at the same moment. The effect is sudden, devastating. An Iraqi battalion suddenly emerges from hiding, still full of fight. Papa Bear is immediately engaged by the lead elements of two enemy armored brigades.

Capt. Ed Ray and his platoon of light armored TOW vehicles from Bravo Company set up shop back at the CP, as ordered, but he's still pretty angry about the assignment in the quiet, safe rear echelon. At 0700, in a thick fog, Colonel Hodory, Task Force Papa Bear commander, is in the process of giving an orders brief when he notices that the audience isn't paying him much attention. They are beginning to hit the deck, and some are preparing weapons to fire. The colonel looks around the corner of the Humvee. A tank force appears out of the gloom where tanks are not supposed to be, about sixty meters away. It is an enemy T-55, moving directly at the CP, gun tube aimed at the cluster of vehicles.

A white flag is noticed, and the tank isn't destroyed. Its commander turns out to be the commanding officer of a regiment of Iraqi tanks. He wants to quit, but they don't. They're right down the road behind him, on their way. The commander provides their radio frequencies but refuses the unit's passwords. A translator gets on the radio asking the Iraqis to quit, but they refuse and turn off their sets.

An Apache's battle position is just above the terrain. This one is owned by the 2nd Armored Division's 1st Battalion, 3rd Attack Helicopter Brigade, the "Gremlins." They fought attached to the 1st Cav. Hans Halberstadt

The rest of the Iraqi force arrives shortly thereafter, emerging from the fog and blasting away. A nearby Marine tank unit gets a call for help, but they too are being engaged by elements of the enemy brigade.

Captain Ray's reinforced platoon of light armored vehicles and a platoon of Humvees with TOW missile launchers get busy. Dragon missiles add to the excitement. Tank rounds blast through the CP area, machine gun bullets kick up dirt around the command element's feet. As the fog lifts, two companies of Marine tanks come on line, taking out enemy vehicles. Eight Cobra attack helicopters arrive to help, launching Hellfire missiles on laser-designated targets. The enemy tanks thrash around for two hours, a few finally escaping the way they had come. The captain stops complaining. His unit kills more than thirty-five enemy armored vehicles within 400–500 meters of the

division CP. More than seventy are killed on the position.

To the southeast, Papa Bear has what is probably the largest armor battle in the history of the Marine Corps. Between 150 and 180 enemy tanks and personnel carriers are destroyed. The marines suffer no casualties.

TF Shepherd's Charlie Company in the Al Burqan oil field gets into a running fight that lasts more than thirty hours, although it is difficult for anyone to sense the passage of time. Flashlights are required to read maps at midday, the sky still black with smoke. Enemy armor blunder around in the desert, individually and without either coordination or support, searching for marines to kill. In the process, they present themselves for slaughter. One of Charlie Company's platoon leaders destroys more than twenty enemy vehicles and captures the enemy com-

An AH–64 Apache helicopter with a full load of laser-guided Hellfire missiles. Department of Defense

68

mander, a colonel. The fight pitted a company of marines against a brigade of Iraqis, and the brigade is destroyed.

Sergeant Zickafoose, one of the heroes of day one, seems to have the right stuff for day two, as well. The Iraqis counterattack his unit's command post with infantry and armor. The sergeant grabs an AT-4 anti-tank weapon and bunker buster and takes off through the smoke and the tracers. He works up close to the right flank of one of the enemy tanks and fires the AT-4, killing the tank and taking the steam out of the enemy attack.

Cpl. Bryan Freeman, a scout team leader, was waiting patiently for Marine Task Force X-ray to be delivered by helicopter when an Iraqi mechanized brigade dropped in instead. Firing became heavy, targets appearing momentarily through the clouds of smoke covering the battlefield. Freeman and his team dash to the battalion's flank to provide security. Three tanks are moving in front of them, 2,500 meters out. The corporal lases them, calls in air strikes, and two are destroyed by Hellfire missiles.

He takes the team off on another dash, toward the loudest sound of guns, and finds two more tanks. Both are lased; one is killed and the other escapes. Freeman now sees an anti-aircraft system far to the front, about 7,000 meters from his position and too far to engage with his laser designator. So off they go again, this time to get closer to the enemy vehicle. They move about 1,000 meters, call for air support,

Possibly the victim of an Apache attack, a destroyed Iraqi tank rusts in the desert. USMC

and designate the target for a Cobra helicopter. The anti-aircraft system is converted to yet another pile of junk on the desert. During all this bullets whiz past the corporal and his team, but they don't seem to care.

Midday of day two, the Marines decide that fun time is over, and back to the serious business of moving on Kuwait City. The sky is so dark at midday that flashlights are required to read maps, night-vision goggles are required to see.

Shepherd moves forward about 1300, runs into a huge ammunition storage area. Iraqi soldiers begin surrendering in large numbers, and Shepherd's advance is effectively stopped by the mass of humanity.

When some of the Iraqis look around and notice how few Marine armored vehicles have defeated them, some seem to change their minds and turn back

for weapons. Bursts of gunfire over their heads bring them back to the fold, however, and they decide to surrender, after all.

TF Grizzly is trucked up to Al Jaber airfield. After clearing the airfield and its buildings, Grizzly sets up a POW compound.

British 4th and 7th Brigades

The British 4th Brigade includes the 14/20 King's Royal Hussars, 1st Royal Scots, 3rd Royal Regiment of Fusilliers and 2nd Field Artillery Regiment. The 4th Brigade's mission will be to follow the American 1st Infantry though the breach, then attack with all of the British 1st Armoured Division up along the heavily defended Wadi Al Batin, swing east across the wadi and through the center of Kuwait toward Kuwait City.

Iraqi bunker complex formerly owned by 2nd Battalion, 45th Iraqi Infantry Division. It has been acquired by the 101st Airborne Division, and is now open under the new *management of Alpha Company, 1st Battalion, 327th Infantry Regiment. US Army*

The Hussars' Challenger tanks get through the breach late on the second day after much frustration and waiting for American units to clear. The Hussars form the vanguard for the main body of the brigade, moving up a route called axis Hawk; the rest follow 1st Battalion, the Royal Scots along axis Tartan, about 1930 hours. It is inky black, raining heavily and so many vehicles crowd the landscape that it looks like the rush hour from hell. The 4th Brigade's mission is the destruction of an enemy artillery brigade to the east. The enemy includes elements of the Iraqi 52nd Armored Brigade on the east of the objective, an infantry battle group on the west and a heavy armor battle group in the middle.

Around midnight, the Challengers find Iraqi tanks moving to their front and flanks. The rain pours down, mixed with soot and ash—the mother of all dark and stormy nights. The T-55 tanks show clearly in the Challengers' thermal sights, well within range. One after another the Iraqi tanks hit and explode in massive fireballs as their ammunition explodes. Turrets fly up into the night, trailing fire, then drop ruined to the battlefield.

Illumination rounds are put into the soggy sky ahead of the lead elements of the Hussars. White flags appear. The Hussars' infantry, the Queen's Company of Grenadiers, "debuss" their Warrior armored personnel carriers and move up cautiously to take the prisoners in.

To the north, flanking the 4th Brigade, the 7th Brigade (Royal Scots Dragoon Guards, 1st Staffordshire Regiment, Queen's Royal Irish Hussars, and the 40th Field Artillery Regiment) attack in parallel.

To the south, the 1st Royal Scots with three infantry companies and one of tanks was heavily engaged with a battalion of Iraqis on objective Bronze. They attack with heavy applications of 30-mm. cannon fire from the Warrior's Rarden gun. Another unit, the Life Guards, provide support with 120-mm. main gunfire from Challenger tanks and heavy machine guns. After a few minutes the Iraqis surrender in droves.

Attack of the Gremlins and Angels

The 1st Cav spends the night in the Wadi Al Batin and on the morning of the second day is still trying to convince the Iraqis that they are going to be hit hardest up the wadi. While far to the west the two huge corps attack against mild opposition, the 1st Cav has lots of enemy targets. And the targets are shooting back with everything they've got.

There are more than enough bunkers, fire trenches and artillery tubes to keep Colonel House's brigade entertained, so to put the lid on two of the

A Black Hawk carries a 105-mm. howitzer to a new position. Hans Halberstadt

71

largest defensive complexes, an attack by the Cav's own helicopters is launched. Thirty-six Apaches go over the task force. The 2nd Brigade shoots a SEAD mission for them, and they prowl forward.

The 1st Cavalry Division, like all the others, has its own private little air force in the form of attack helicopter battalions, 1/3 and 1/227. These units fly older, upgraded Cobras with wire-guided TOW missiles and 20-mm. guns and the more modern Apache, with its laser-guided Hellfires and 30-mm. gun. Both get a workout, tasked with contingency missions to defend against counterattacks, screening missions, and providing security for logistical sites, in addition to attacking enemy armor and other units in the open. Their call signs are Gremlin, Angel, and Steel.

The Cav sends its Apache scouts forward of its advance up the Wadi Al Batin to deal with a dug-in defensive position. For the helicopter pilots, the pucker factor is high; doctrine and training emphasize night operations over day in attacks against mobile, exposed enemy. The mission, though, is in daylight. The enemy is dug in with lots of air defense artillery and missile systems.

They've been waiting for this moment for four and a half months, and they're tired of the desert, the sand, the alerts, the nuclear, biological, chemical

A CH–47 Chinook ferries equipment and supplies deep into Iraq on day two of the land war. US Army/Maj. Kuenning

72

(NBC) suits, and especially the waiting. As they prepare for their first real combat, the pilots report a mixture of strong emotions: excitement, fear, anticipation, and relief that the waiting is finally over.

Some of the pilots are from 1st Battalion, 3rd Attack Helicopter Brigade; they call themselves Gremlins. And the enemy soldiers on their objective must feel as if they've been visited by a horde of evil, invisible gremlins on the morning of day two.

They attack in a long line, with about 1,000 m. between each of the six helicopters, with the sun behind them. The gunners acquire targets, launching Hellfire missiles from four miles away in the first phase of the attack. For some of the pilots, this is the first time they've actually launched a live missile. But on the little green television display in the cockpit, Gremlin gunners watch in fascination as Iraqi tanks explode in massive fireballs.

This particular group of enemy soldiers wants to wait awhile before they quit, and in the meantime, they start launching everything they've got at the attacking helicopters as they move in on the position and become exposed.

After taking out the tanks, some of the Apaches press in on the position, shooting up bunkers, trucks, BDRM personnel carriers, and anything else that looks interesting. In the process, they're exposed to some very annoyed enemy soldiers who greet them with fire from personal weapons, anti-aircraft cannon, heat seeking missiles, and—no doubt—a few unkind words. Artillery is called in on the Gremlins, too, and the pilots start moving the helicopters around to avoid the bursts nearby.

One of the hazards of flying attack helicopters in daylight against dug-in adversaries is that you become far more vulnerable to all kinds of weapons. For the Gremlins, this means a lot of small arms fire, anti-aircraft cannon, and missile fire directed at the helicopters. The Apache has, fortunately, a suite of countermeasure systems and armor that can help deflect some of the threats.

"Sitting in your firing position, you were very conscious of rockets and small arms being fired at you. You could see the SA-14 and -16 IR missiles launched," one of the pilots reports, "and you could see them coming! They'd go right over the top of you, or off to one side. That's when you say your prayers, and thank whoever built the IR jammer."

Soviet-built missiles start whizzing up to greet the Gremlins. Most are "spoofed" by the infrared (IR) jammer on the helicopter and only damage the pilot's peace of mind. But one of the Apaches from a sister battalion isn't so lucky. They've been extra aggressive and have worked up closer to the enemy positions, taking on tanks and anti-aircraft positions, and one of the Iraqis decides to return the favor. The Apache takes a missile squarely behind the pilot's seat, through the number two engine, and down it goes, thrashing out of control.

The $10 million helicopter is a total loss, but one of the things the designers incorporated was protection for the crew in moments like this. The Apache, as one pilot says, crashes *really* well. The airframe absorbs the shock, as advertised, and the priceless pilots are salvageable. One of their compadres drops out of the sky to provide a lift. Both are okay, and are able to climb on the Apache's landing gear and hold on for a ride back to safety. Their rescuers will get Bronze Stars, complete with a little V for valor. The rescued pilots hop in to a fresh Apache, and dive back into the war.

Before the war, Hellfire missiles were too expensive to actually fire in training, and few of the pilots have ever had the opportunity to launch one. But more than fifty Hellfires are launched in the engage-

The Royal Scots, 7th Brigade, 1st (British) Armoured Division press on into Iraq on day two. For the British, the first day was hurry-up-and-wait for the American 1st Infantry Division to get out of the damn way. The 7th Brigade are the famous "Desert Rats." The entire British 1st Armoured was among the most professional and competent of the units deployed, highly respected by American soldiers. USN

ment. They kill four tanks, eight BDRMs, lots of artillery, bunkers and other targets. The pilots watch enemy soldier run into bunkers, followed by a Hellfire and a huge explosion. One pilot fires on a tank, then notices a crewman standing in the turret; when the missile hits, half of him goes one way, half goes another.

The 30-mm. gun also gets a workout. While not as glamorous or dramatic as the rockets or missile systems, the gun turns out to be a star performer. "The gun was really impressive," a pilot says. "We used the high explosive dual purpose rounds, with depleted uranium core, and it was very effective. We were hitting very accurately at 2,500 m., and even got them out to 4,000 m.!" The enemy infantry pop their heads up out of trenches long enough to get off bursts of small arms fire and be fired on in return. The Apache fire control system is tied into the pilot's helmet, through a complicated system of sensors, computers, and a little screen that sits in front of the pilot's right eye. But with the right switches in the right positions, the gun will aim wherever the pilot looks. All he has to do is look out of the cockpit, find a target, and squeeze the trigger to engage enemy soldiers. So while the

gunner up front is busy with the missiles, the pilot in back is looking for infantry.

"Somebody would poke their head up and shoot—and they wouldn't shoot anymore!" says the pilot.

The raiders withdraw. The 2nd Brigade is ordered to destroy what's left of the crashed helicopter, just to make sure none of its black boxes end up in the wrong hands. A platoon drives up to the smoldering battlefield and launches a TOW missile into the carcass of the Apache. The resulting explosion scatters $10 million worth of high technology across a desert already littered with billions worth of scrap metal.

The 2nd Brigade's commander, Colonel House, gets a call from his boss, the division commander, wanting to know if the wadi is a safe route after all.

"We're dancing scouts out, tanks are firing, the artillery battalion is firing more direct support artillery than anywhere in theater, going through minefields, busting down defensive positions—taking fire, returning fire, killing this outfit and that outfit. But the further I went north, the thicker the battlefield got. I was absolutely convinced they were going to get my whole brigade up in these fire traps and then

American and French equipment and supplies push on into Iraq on day two. Kirby Lee Vaughn

hit us with chemical. My mission was to find out if there was a soft spot, without getting attritted. Finally, at noon of the 25th I called the CG and said, 'Sir, I can get through this complex—but it *ain't* soft!'"

The brigade is pulled back out of the wadi, refueled, and prepared to attack the next day.

101st Airborne

Early on the morning of G Plus 1, the 3rd Brigade of the 101st Airborne air assaults deep into enemy territory again. This time, it is all the way up in the Euphrates river valley, just across the river from the city of As Samawah where the battle maps have been inscribed area of operations (AO) Eagle. A four-lane highway is the only road available for the Iraqis to move east or west on this side of the Euphrates, and now it is blocked by the 3rd Brigade.

The road is cratered with explosives. The brigade sets up a kill zone along the highway, waiting for enemy convoys. And they don't have long to wait before a supply convoy shows up. The lead truck even has its headlights on—making it a conspicuous target. In an effort to get the truck drivers to stop and surrender, a machine gun fires tracers in front of the lead vehicle, but it speeds up rather than stops. An AT-4 anti-tank rocket is fired into the cab, blowing it apart and stopping the truck and the whole convoy.

Daylight reveals the cargo, a large quantity of onions, scattered over a wide area. Soon Bedouin tribe members arrive to loot the convoy, which turns out to be entirely food for Iraqi soldiers. The soldiers try to scare the Bedouin off by shooting over their heads, but it doesn't work. So they give up on that tactic and proceed to help them pack up the food, just to get them out of the kill zone.

24th Mech Infantry

It's a long drive across Iraq for the 24th and 197th to their first objective, labeled Grey on the battle maps. To get there the force crosses a landscape that

An Apache ready to go on the warpath, way out west in the XVIII Corps sector. Department of Defense

reminds them of a soggy Grand Canyon, full of deep wadis and steep cliffs, but with swamps mixed in for variety. And while navigating up one of the wadis, one of the company teams has its first encounter with the much-feared, battle hardened foe. They have their hands up before a shot is fired. "They were miserable," a captain says, "they didn't have any food or water, anything to wear, they were ready to give up." The prisoners keep thanking their captors. Some say, "What took you so long?" Others are convinced that they will be killed, but no longer care and just want to get it over with. This is not exactly the kind of engagement the task force was expecting, but they give the POWs food and water and head them to a collection point in the rear.

Reports from other units indicate that occasional POWs are still willing to fight, and there are incidents where Americans are hurt. Everybody is on edge. Still, prisoners are being taken and processed. But in the night a tragedy befalls the 3/15 Inf task force: a grenade goes off, apparently by accident, killing two and badly injuring two others. They are the first casualties for the battalion.

197th Brigade

Midnight finds the 197th Brigade deep into Iraq, screening the invisible 24th Infantry somewhere over

Rush hour traffic at the border. Alpha Company, 299th Engineer Battalion breach the berm for their business associates. US Army/Sp. Henry

76

to the left. Scouts and helicopters report no enemy contact, and the advance thunders forward. Just short of the first objective, code named Brown, the task force pauses to refuel, then moves on. The Air Force provides support with a few loads of bombs. "It was like being at a fireworks display," one major remembers, "with all of the troops standing on top of their vehicles clapping and yelling. Then we got the order to move, and we took off into the night. We took the objective just after first light and captured 49 enemy. They didn't want to fight. We captured a lot of equipment, a lot of supplies."

For many of the soldiers in the personnel carriers, the advance isn't exciting at all, after the border is crossed. Some had been on combat patrols for days previous, with three and four hour's sleep a night. As the hours and the miles roll by, they start to fall asleep. The objective for the 197th is to cut a highway that is unofficially called Scud Road. Not only has it been used for moving missiles, but there's a good chance the enemy forces will want to use it to react to the attacking coalition forces. The objective area contains buildings that may house a supply point. After taking Objective Brown, elements of the task force set up battle positions for a possible enemy counterattack, while other elements dash down the highway toward the west, linking up with the 101st Airborne.

By midmorning of day two the brigade is resting in defensive positions, but by late afternoon, after being refueled, they're moving again. The next objective will be an attack position overlooking the Euphrates river valley. They get to eat an MRE and most catch two or three hour's sleep, then mount up again and move out into a gathering storm. According to the plan, there are two lines of advance. But one proves entirely impassable, and the other nearly so. The entire brigade snakes through the gloom, across the enemy landscape, in one long and vulnerable line. The 2nd Battalion, 69th Armor leads the force up a little track in the wilderness. They drive on into the gathering night. They've been attacking for 48 hours, and the adrenalin is wearing off. They're tired.

Sitrep, Day Two

As the second day of the ground campaign concludes, XVIII Corps has swept deep into Iraq, taken control of the Euphrates river valley, and is charging east toward Basra and the Republican Guards. VII Corps is poised to enter Kuwait's western border and to fight the heavily armored mobile tactical reserve divisions from their flank. 1st and 2nd Marine Division task forces are on line north of a line between Al Jaber and the Burqan; they haven't moved far, but they destroyed masses of the enemy. And, they have pressed up close to Kuwait International Airport, now only a few kilometers to the north. Saudi units have moved 25 mi. up the coast and threaten Kuwait City. Egyptian, Kuwaiti, Qatari and Syrian forces have pressed up to 50 mi., now close in on Kuwait City from the west. All units are far ahead of schedule.

Casualties during the attack remain light, but far to the rear, a Scud warhead lands on a converted warehouse where many recent arrivals are billeted. Twenty-eight soldiers die; ninety are injured. Among the dead are Beverly Clark, a 23-year-old specialist who loved to ski. William Palmer dies that day, too, entering Kuwait. The casualties are light only if none are your friends.

Saddam Hussein broadcasts an order over Baghdad Radio for his troops to leave Kuwait.

On the evening of G Plus 1 the 1st Battalion of the 7th Marines are relieved by the 3rd Battalion, and move out from Al Jaber airfield toward their assault positions for their next objective, Kuwait International Airport. Smoke from burning oil wells has turned day into the blackest of nights. Two marines from 1st Battalion become casualties when they walk into parked tanks, completely invisible at midday. The marines are still keyed up, alert for enemy counterattacks. "It was the night of the attacking bushes," one lieutenant says. "It took me two hours to walk only 800 meters, and I ended up walking into a tank. It was *that* dark."

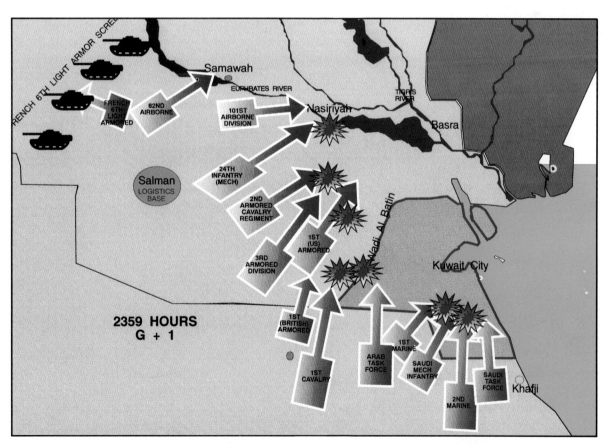

At midnight of the second day, the noose tightens. Much of Iraq's combat power is gone. The Marines and Arab forces are heavily engaged inside Kuwait where the going is slow. To the west the blitzkrieg accelerates, pushing the Iraqis deeper into the trap.

Chapter 5

26 February: G Plus 2

Marines

Midnight of day three finds the Marine 1st Marine Division task forces Ripper, Shepherd, Papa Bear and the rest of the 1st Marine Expeditionary Force consolidating their positions facing Kuwait City and Kuwait International airport. The I Marine Division's objective for today will be to secure the airport. The 2nd Marine Division's objective is the little suburb to the west of Kuwait City, a town called Al Jahra, west of the airport; taking it will block the escape of retreating enemy forces leaving the capital.

Lt. Col. Clifford Myers III of Task Force Shepherd gets the nod to move up to the airport, establish a screen line to the east. They move out about 1500. Shepherd's Charlie Company is still fighting in the Burqan and is ordered to disengage. They do, but kill another six tanks first.

As the marines move up to the outskirts of Kuwait City, they are occasionally taken under fire by enemy tanks, but the enemy action continues to be uncoordinated and ineffective. Gunners scan the night for targets. Enemy vehicles with engines running show up bright in the thermal sights and are destroyed one by one.

Enemy T-72 tanks have been attempting to engage all night, without luck. The marines continue to attack through and past any light resistance. The tactic continues to produce floods of prisoners; they are pointed to the rear and march off by themselves. Colonel Cole: "I attribute our success to our approach, to affect the enemy's will to fight and to make sure

A tank driver from the 24th Infantry Division. On G Plus 2, the 24th pushed deeper into Iraq, driving hard toward Nasiriyah. US Army

that he did not want to fight. And, throughout the battle, the attempt to get behind him, beating him up on the flanks with fire support while attacking forward . . . make him more and more irrelevant to the whole process. The attempt to affect his will and the method we used to wage the battle was not designed to destroy every enemy, but at defeating his will to fight."

Out west, the two huge armored corps are still charging across the desert. The last two days have brought them up to the Euphrates River, trapping the Iraqi army. Today, XVIII Airborne and VII Corps will turn to the east, toward a confrontation with the dangerous Republican Guards and their hundreds of tanks. The marines waiting to storm the beaches of Kuwait are still aboard their ships in the gulf.

Deep in Iraq, an enemy commander knows that today he will be attacked by the British 1st Armoured Division. He orders them to fight to the death. They do, in a way; they kill him and prepare to surrender.

British 4th and 7th Brigades

On G Plus 2 the British continue the attack toward Kuwait City, east to west. The going here is slow. Inside their Warrior armored personnel carriers some of the infantry sleep as their battlefield bus rocks and rolls across the terrain. There is nothing for them to do, to see, or even to hear except the roar of the engine, the rumble of the tracks and the laconic, formal conversations on the radios.

Before dawn, to the north, 7th Brigade's Alpha Company, the 1st Staffordshire Regiment, is on objective Copper where the Iraqis have a communication facility. Before them is a long trench complex. Out of the trench comes machine gun bullets. Iraqi tanks and APCs are dug in around the trench; soldiers run around without organization or purpose, firing. The Staffordshires fire up the place, killing all visible armor.

Alpha Company's infantry debuss to clear the complex. An Iraqi pops up, fires at Pvt. Mark Eason. He feels a powerful jolt to the chest and is knocked to the ground, screaming for a medic. While waiting for his short life to come to its end, Private Eason starts exploring his damaged body for the awful wound, but can't seem to find it. After a few moments he notices that the magazine for his rifle has been smashed by a bullet but he is unholed. Private Eason gets up and carries on with the trench clearing.

Light begins to filter through the smog over the battlefield. The 7th Brigade brings up a psyops (psychological operations) team with loudspeakers. Five hundred Iraqis immediately surrender.

The British commander, Brig. Patrick Cordingley, orders the troops to encourage surrender with warning shots rather than direct fire against troops in the open.

At 0900, 7th Brigade attacks with 4th Brigade. The 1st Staffordshire Regiment leads, helicopter scouts forward offering friendly advice on land navigation. They charge through enemy positions, avoiding strong points identified by the helicopters, taking out enemy positions from the flanks and the rear.

At 0930, the 14/20 Hussars charge east toward a new objective marked "Brass" on the battle maps. The charge lasts two hours, devouring dozens of enemy tanks, personnel carriers, trucks and armored vehicles. The Hussars pull to a halt on Brass and are overwhelmed by Iraqi soldiers desperate to surrender.

The M1 Abrams' driver's position. The driver reclines, steers with the T handle, and is usually "buttoned up." Then he sees the outside world through a periscope and a thermal imager. The transmission is automatic, the acceleration rapid. If you can drive a kiddie car, you can drive a tank. Hans Halberstadt

4th Brigade attacks objective Bronze at 1045. They attack under a drenching artillery prep by the Brigade's 2nd Field Artillery Regiment on the enemy positions, and the prep continues while the 4th Brigade's leading elements roll up to the objective. The infantry debuss and clean the trenches with grenades, rifles and CLAW close assault weapon. It is over by noon.

By afternoon, day three, the Staffordshires find hordes of enemy tanks to the front, preparing to counterattack. The Iraqi tanks are hunted down, one at a time, and taken out with main guns and Milan anti-tank missiles.

The British have always liked their Challenger main battle tank in training; they *love* it in combat. They claim its gun is even more accurate than the M1A1 Abrams', and one of the Royal Scots Dragoon Guards elects to test his on the battlefield. He finds an enemy tank, "hot" in his thermal sight, 5,100 meters (more than three miles) away—one shot, one tank kill.

The fight takes hours. When it's finished, 7th Brigade, Staffordshires forward, attack east again toward a new objective and a new enemy concentration. The objective is called Lead, and the enemy is a well-emplaced Iraqi battalion of mechanized infantry.

An M1 tank commander. The commander is usually a sergeant—a good one, with maturity, judgment, initiative and lots of experience. He stands or sits. If standing, he can see well but is exposed to enemy fire. If sitting, he is safer but has limited visibility. The commander can take control of the gun from the gunner with his override; he also has a heavy machine gun of his own. Hans Halberstadt

When the Brigade reaches Lead, a long, ripping burst of machine gun fire over the position invites the enemy to come out like good boys and play nice. Some do; some don't. Charlie Company debusses its Warriors to deal with the prisoners. While they're busy taking names and numbers, a renegade group of Iraqis form up to counterattack. A heavy machine gun fires on Charlie Company. A rocket-propelled grenade is fired at one of the Warriors, but hits Pvt. Steven Moult first. He is killed instantly. The RPG sets fire to the Warrior, injuring the commander. The gunner, Guardsman Darren Chant, pulls the commander out and extinguishes the fire.

Elsewhere on the objective, a 16/5 Lancers recon element and Alpha Squadron and Queen's Dragoon Guards, get in a fight that lasts into the night. The British are on the edge of the Wadi Al Batin, ready to invade Kuwait.

Day three is a sad one for 4th Brigade and the British 1st Armoured Division. An American A-10 fires on two Warriors, destroying both. Nine troopers of the 3rd Royal Regiment of Fusilliers and Queen's Own Highlanders are killed, eleven wounded.

The British are facing the Iraqi Medina and Hamarabi divisions of the Republican Guards. These are the enemy's best, a strategic reserve force with all the good stuff the Iraqi army owns—including lots of T-72 tanks. Electronic warfare system intercepts indicate these two divisions will come out of their holes to protect the enemy withdrawal to the north. Out of their bunkers, the Republican Guards will finally become the kind of targets the British and allies have been waiting for.

Near dusk, 4th Brigade gets a mission to attack an artillery complex defending the Wadi Al Batin. Fusilliers and Royal Scots take the lead. At last light their attack kicks off, fifty-four Challenger tanks up front with the heavy combat power. The tanks cross the line of departure for the attack, a high sand berm over an oil pipeline. Behind, an artillery prep is fired. Two regiments of tube artillery and two rocket batteries fire for ten minutes, drenching the objective area with steel.

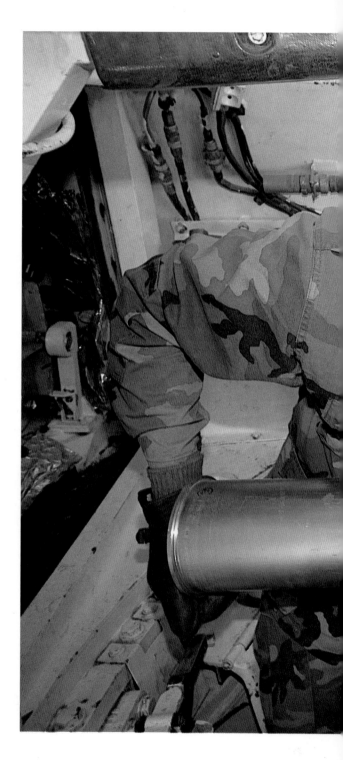

The M1 loader. The main gun rounds are stored behind doors that isolate them from the turret in case of fire. When needed, the loader uses his knee to operate the door switch, then punches the base of the selected round with his fist, and it springs out at him. The round is slid from the rack, swapped end for end and shoved into the breech. The breech block slams shut and the loader calls, "Up!" Hans Halberstadt

When the Scots and Fusilliers arrive on the objective they are greeted with raised arms and only occasional small arms fire. In a headquarters complex they find elaborate preparations for defense against an attack that never came—the one up the Wadi from the south. The complex is well stocked with the South African G-5 artillery piece, probably the best heavy gun made.

After a pause, the British brigades are alerted to prepare to fight the two Iraqi reserve divisions the Hamarabi and the Medina, now reported moving. The 7th Brigade leads and the 4th follows through the wadi, squadrons on line. The King's Royal Hussars find targets at long range and fire them up. The targets turn out to be Spartan command vehicles from 10th Air Defense Battery, in the wrong place at the wrong time. Fortunately the crews were out of the vehicles

when they were hit and no one was hurt. The charge continues into the gathering gloom. The Republican Guards threat disappears in the gloom.

Inside Kuwait city, Iraqi soldiers are in a frenzy of looting and destruction. Vehicles are stolen, loaded with any available booty, and driven north. Enemy command and control seems to have broken down entirely. There is still resistance from isolated pockets, particularly Republican Guards units, but most Iraqis are simply running for their lives or surrendering at the first chance. Outside the city, a traffic jam of military and stolen private vehicles clogs the highway for miles. Above the jam, Air Force A-10 Warthog close air support aircraft orbit, waiting their turns to fire.

Marines of Task Force Ripper will participate in the mission for today, to seize Kuwait International

The M1 Abrams' gunner's station. It's crowded in here. The gunner sights through an eyepiece and aims the gun with the grip controls. The computer—which needs to be *told what kind of ammunition is being loaded and a few other tidbits—is to his right. When ready to fire the gunner calls, "On the way!"* Hans Halberstadt

Airport, and everybody is ready to go at 0600. The attack is delayed for half an hour because of minimal visibility. The burning oil wells impede the assault, make life difficult for the attackers, but at 0630 on G Plus 2 the drivers of several hundred 7th Marine Expeditionary Force tanks, Humvees, trucks, Amtracks and associated vehicles shift into gear, release brakes, and Ripper starts moving again.

For the 7th Marines, attacking to the west of the airport, the resistance begins to stiffen. Lead elements of 1st Battalion encounter a large quarry complex that doesn't appear on their maps. The area is full of little wadis, fissures, and hiding places for defenders. Artillery is fired into the area to suppress any loyal defenders, and the advance continues. Cobra attack

helicopters prowl overhead, find a few enemy BMPs and T-62 tanks, engage them with TOW missiles and 20-mm. cannon fire. The Cobra pilots report all clear, and the marines drive on.

As the lightly armored trucks of the field trains come in range of the quarry they are engaged by a few die-hard defenders still hidden in the rocks. For the marines it is the hairiest moment of the campaign because the anti-tank teams are now engaged forward. But the low visibility and limited range of the enemy guns protects the force long enough for several TOW gunners and M 60 tanks to find targets in their thermal sights.

It is just the kind of engagement for which the marines have been rehearsing, some for an entire

101st Airborne soldiers with a trusty 105-mm. howitzer, the infantryman's friend in time of need. US Army

career. TOW missiles are expensive, so the gunners have been practicing with glorified video games called simulators. Each of the gunners has fired at BMPs and T-62s dozens or hundreds of times before as images on a screen. It isn't a complicated process: identify the target, put the cross-hairs of the thermal sight sensor on the center of mass, arm and launch the missile. Now all you have to do is keep the cross-hairs centered on the target until the missile impacts. That's how it works with the simulator, and that's how it works on the way to Kuwait International—almost.

On the real battlefield the TOW gunner finds things a little different from the simulator version. For one thing, the engagement begins when a real target tries to kill the gunner or one of his friendly associates. For another, when a real TOW is launched, it is with a huge tongue of flame that identifies the gunner to everyone on the battlefield. The target has about ten seconds to react—an eternity in combat—and if the TOW gunner can be hit or just distracted for a moment (a near miss will usually do) the missile will miss. Added to that are all the uncertainties and stresses of combat, the hazards of shooting at a friendly unit, all of which make the gunner's job a difficult one in ways the simulator can't replicate. According to one Marine platoon leader: "We had 3rd Tank Battalion off to our left, something moving out in front of us, friendlies ways off to our right, so I told the

Oil fields burn in Kuwait. The fires could have been set out of simple spite, or to prevent coalition forces from seeing Iraqi targets. While the smoke created some problems for the coalition forces during the assault, it made *things much worse for the Iraqis. Since they had few thermal imaging systems to see through the smoke, they were blinded by their own actions. USAF/T. Sgt. Heimer*

gunners 'you can't engage unless you can positively identify an enemy vehicle or it fires at you,' and we met both those criteria."

While peering through the gloom, the platoon leader spots a shape maneuvering off to the right, near the quarry site, where no friendly forces are supposed to be. It looks like a T-62, about 1,000 meters away, which then fires its main gun. A HEAT round explodes only fifty meters from the lieutenant's unarmored humvee, spattering it with shrapnel, and the enemy tank's coaxial machine gun adds to the excitement with a long burst. The TOW gunner decides that the platoon leader's rules of engagement have been properly met, and launches his missile, which departs with a flash and a roar. The gunners manning the heavy .50-caliber machine guns on vehicles nearby open up, hosing the offending target and the surrounding area with fire. The marines watch the missile dance downrange, its bright red thermal tracker clearly visible. The TOW seems to jump around, bobbing as its small sustainer rockets fire to correct its course through the gloom. Then, impact and the tank comes violently apart at the seams as the ammunition inside explodes.

Alpha Company finds a bunker complex and the TOW vehicles spread out in a huge arc and begin to engage. "At the beginning you could see some green tracers coming back, but that didn't last very long," one of the sergeants remembers. "It was unreal," says another. "You didn't realize people were dying in there. The TOWs were going off, and they were getting 'catastrophic kills' all over the place. That means that every time a tank blows up, three or four people die. But at those ranges, it seemed abstract in a way,

Fires of a different kind: Iraqi tanks burn in the desert after a demoralizing tank dual with American Abrams tanks. USMC

unreal." They see one dead soldier, a tank crewman who didn't quite make it out of his burning tank, his hands still holding the grips of the heavy machine gun he was firing.

For the infantry it is all very confusing. "We had TOWs right behind us," one platoon leader says, "and they start yelling. They had enemy tanks in sight, but we couldn't see anything! So they shot, and we *still* couldn't see anything . . . and we'd wait, and wait, and finally BOOM! We'd see flames and they start yelling again and here comes another one: BANG! That kept up for maybe a half an hour or 45 minutes and we still couldn't see anything." The marines' missiles can outrange the enemy tank guns, which are only accurate out to 1,000 meters.

The behavior of the Iraqi tanks is odd. "They didn't do anything we expected," one sergeant says. "These guys are Soviet-trained. Their doctrine calls for certain things they're supposed to do when they're getting shot at by a TOW gunner—and these guys didn't do them. They shot back at us, not real accurately, and they kept moving, but they didn't do their immediate action drills that we expected. I don't know if they were ill-trained or scared or what."

The 2nd Battalion, 3rd Marines were attacking toward their final, ultimate objective, Kuwait International Airport. Along their advance roared the flames of scores of burning oil wells, the fires reaching hundreds of feet into the air. All around the vehicles was destruction and the bizarre, frightening land-

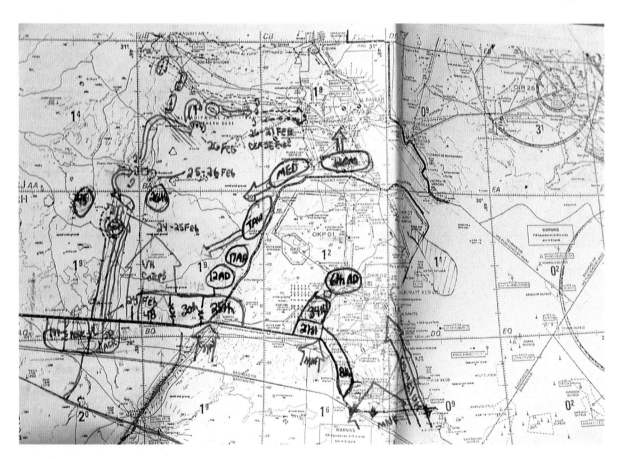

A battle map used by Captain Sutherland, Bravo Company commander, 3rd Battalion, 15th Infantry Brigade, 24th Infantry Division on the 24th's push toward the Euphrates. The 24th's route is shown in blue. Enemy movements are shown in red. Hans Halberstadt

scape, the sky black with smoke. But Marines have a unique way of looking at things, so over the battalion radios came a call from one of the company commanders: "Immediate resupply of marshmallows!"

The marines move to engage under skies inky black with smoke, reading maps by flashlight and relying on thermal sights to find the enemy. The M1A1 Abrams tank can out-range the T-72, so Marine tanks quickly pull back out of their effective range and start to engage. The Iraqi rounds fall hundreds of meters from their targets, making fountains of sand and dirt. The marines' rounds hit squarely on the enemy turrets, creating fountains of fire.

The tank battle lasts all day, between the marines' old, reliable M60 tanks and the Iraqis' T-55, T-62 and modern T-72 tanks. Once again, the thermal sights and accurate fire control systems of the coalition armor out-classes the opposition. Dust and smoke prevent enemy gunners from engaging the marines effectively, their shots falling short or going wide. But one after another, the Iraqi armor takes sabot and HEAT rounds. The airport becomes cluttered with the blazing wrecks of destroyed tanks, over 300 in all. By evening the airport is secured. The entire enemy force is destroyed. Not a single Marine tank has been put out of action by enemy guns.

But the marines don't get away unhurt. L. Cpl. Brian Lane, a twenty-year-old, is killed in the fight for the airport. Marine L. Cpl. Christian Porter goes down nearby. There are many more wounded. After seventy-two hours of combat, the marines have lost 5 killed and 48 wounded.

Elements of the 7th Marines drive on, taking ground around the airport to provide security. Past the airport they encounter more obstacles and mines. The line charges are again put to work, blowing lanes through. The 1st Battalion halts that evening at a position that should be just outside Kuwait City but in the smoky gloom little is visible. The next morning, however, brings a surprise: the city is just a few hundred meters to the front. And another surprise: "Right in front of our position three ZSU-23 anti-aircraft, anti-personnel heavy machine guns, still loaded, and one with the barrels pointed level, straight at us," according to one Marine sergeant, "All anybody needed to do was pull the trigger! We destroyed those guns the next day."

The 1st Marine Light Armored Infantry was moving up toward Kuwait City past streams of enemy prisoners. Many of the Iraqis believed the stories they'd been told about the treatment they could expect if captured, but some believed more than others. One of these was noticed marching southward,

hands up, too frightened to haul up his pants, which had slid to his ankles.

Although Marines have never been shy about encouraging their special legend, the Iraqis apparently were so impressed that they added to it. Many of the POWs reported that they were told that a condition of enlistment in the US Marines involved the murder of a close family member. So when captured by Marines, many enemy prisoners of war (EPWs) expected torture and death.

Alpha Company, 1st LAI, is processing a large number of defectors. As one corporal approaches a group of Iraqis a member of the group asks in English, "Are you US Army?"

"No, we're Marines," the corporal tells them. They immediately fling themselves on the ground, wailing and speaking hysterically among themselves. "You are really Marines?" asks the thoroughly frightened prisoner. "You will kill us now?"

"No, we're going to feed you and give you water. You're out of the war."

"No! You're Marines! You're going to kill us!" The despair lasts until they've been given MREs and water, at which point they finally begin to relax.

Elsewhere, the miserable condition of the prisoners inspires Marines and soldiers to offer special care. One unit sets up its only tent to provide shelter for the EPWs while the marines live and sleep on the wet ground. Other units provide clothing, spare boots, blankets, food, and water—none of which was originally intended for POWs.

The medics, who were expecting to be busy treating allied wounded, instead go to work on the enemy soldiers. Many have severe wounds, others are dehydrated, some are near death from many causes. Watching the treatment, an Iraqi officer told the medics that his men were being treated better as prisoners of the enemy than as their own army.

In return, the gratitude of the captives becomes at times overpowering. Soldiers and marines are kissed by smelly men with soggy mustaches, hardly the reaction anybody expected from an army that had received such good press before the war began.

The coalition forces are nearly overwhelmed with a flood of POWs, and their reaction to capture is not always predictable. Over near the town of Al Jaber, 1st Lt. Rusty Koontz, an officer from 3rd Marines, was using his platoon's fourteen trucks to help move the masses of enemy captives. From out of the crowd of Iraqis comes an American voice: "Hey, do you speak English?" Lieutenant Koontz said he did. The voice replied, "My name is Fred. I'm from Los Angeles. I'm not supposed to be here!" Further investigation revealed that the prisoner had come to Iraq to visit relatives, was conscripted, and made a company commander. When asked if any of the other members of his company spoke English, Fred replied that he had taught them all a little. Each could say "Saddam sucks!"

Elsewhere in the sector, a group of more than seventy enemy present themselves to 2nd Battalion, 7th Marines, hands in the air. One of the POWs advances, waving a piece of paper on which is written:

"We turned ourselves in to 5th Battalion, 11th Marines. We were searched and have no weapons. We have 1 lieutenant, 1 sergeant, and 2 corporals in our group. We were given an MRE and water from 5/11. Aren't they a fine bunch of guys? Especially SSGT ——.

"[signed] SSGT —— S2 Chief, 5/11"

XVIII Airborne Corps

Way out west, day three finds the XVIII Corps continuing its long, fast sweep around the defenses, over 130 miles into Iraq, toward the end of a frantic, epic race across a nightmare battlefield. Casualties have been light, until now, thanks to many factors. The low visibility is certainly one. The speed of the assault is another. The reliability of the equipment is another. But the performance of the soldiers is crucial. The whole task force is thinking of what will happen when they encounter the Republican Guards.

The mission for today is to seize a main highway up ahead, then an attack on Tallil air base to the east.

Tanks and Bradleys squirm and slide across the sodden desert. There is mud everywhere. Sheer cliffs, swamps, hills confront the 197th Infantry, and then,

Thousands of Iraqi tanks like this one were destroyed during the hundred-hour Storm. This one was another victim of the British 1st Armoured Division. USN

at about 0100, it begins to rain. Wind lashes the rain and picks up sand. "It turned into a mudstorm there for a while," one captain says.

At 0500 the commander calls a halt until daylight, hoping visibility improves. Then, at 0630, the attack continues. "We were the lead task force," a captain says, "and we found the route by getting vehicles stuck." The technique is a simple one: as tanks and APCs get stuck, the following vehicles try someplace else, until the next nasty spot gets someone else bogged down. A huge river confronts the brigade where a little wadi is shown on the map. "We got an entire company stuck in the mud at one in the morning, and decided to figure it out when the sun came up in the morning. And when the sun rose it looked like a nuclear bomb had gone off: vehicles facing in all directions, some over on their sides. You'd send two vehicles out to retrieve one and all three would get stuck. It took us all morning just to get out of there."

But elements of the brigade are able to occupy the objective by 1000 on the morning of day three, the assembly area for the attack on Tallil air base that is supposed to begin at 1400. Another sandstorm begins, the worst of the entire deployment. Visibilities are down to five feet, but the task forces still manage to refuel while the commanders plot and scheme. Intel reports indicate large enemy concentrations on the air base. The attack kicks off.

The first encounter happens when Bravo Company 3/15, encounters a huge, well-manned defensive position, and attacks across it. The rolling terrain provides some cover for the assault elements, and since communications for the enemy forces are poor, lots of defenders are caught by total surprise. One

Members of the 3rd Platoon, Alpha Company, 1st Battalion, 327th Parachute Infantry Regiment, 82nd Airborne Division. They've just defeated an Iraqi division—with a little help from their friends. US Army/Sp. Elliot

91

tank rolls up over a sand dune, suddenly confronting three Iraqis. They panic, fall on the ground in frightened surrender. One, an officer, turns out to be a Republican Guard; so much for the legend of the Iraqi elite.

The task force begins taking droves of prisoners, their numbers beginning to cause problems. When the company commander starts looking around the complex it becomes obvious why the enemy is so ready to quit: their food is moldy bread, rain supplies the only water, and their clothing is completely inadequate for the conditions. Even Republican Guards can become miserable. But their weapons are in great shape, and the bunkers are full of ammunition.

"If they would have fought, it would have been real nasty," a sergeant says. "They had good, well-dug-in positions, equipment was well placed, and lots of ammunition. But their morale was completely destroyed."

Weapons are the tools of a soldier's trade, and the AK assault rifles of the Iraqis are excellent, beautiful firearms, perfectly maintained. Captain Sutherland stops to collect the personal weapons of an Iraqi unit. The soldiers gather round to work the bolts, examine

Sp. Shannon Segall displays a captured Iraqi weapon. Kirby Lee Vaughn

92

the quality of the weapons before destroying them. They are admired, then laid out on the ground. A tank is driven across the rifles, bending and crushing them into uselessness. "I took this one officer's AK-M, and it was beautiful, a brand-new weapon, right out of the box. I hated to get rid of it. We let everybody look at them, play with them a little, then we laid them out on the road—and crushed them with the tracks."

And the soldiers start noticing something odd about the ammunition in the bunkers, too. Jordan has been claiming for months to respect the arms embargo imposed by the United Nations on Iraq, but the bunkers are full of crates of small arms ammunition with Jordanian labels. The dates on the crates are January 1991. And, in English, the legend "From your Arab brothers in Jordan." So much for the arms embargo.

The advance has been so fast and so far into Iraq that the Bradleys and tanks begin running out of gas. Most make it to the refuel point on fumes. And just before the task force is scheduled to begin another attack, a young supply officer shows up with 25,000 gallons of fuel. Captain Sutherland:

"The problem now became fuel! The day of the 26th, as we were closing in on the Euphrates River Valley, into BP 103 and 104, for the attack on Jalibah Airfield, fuel became critical. I had taken 30,000 gallons of fuel with me on this march and had used it all up. So I sent my Support Platoon leader, a young lieutenant, and told him: 'Go south. Get fuel. Meet me north. I don't know where I'll be.' I told him that early in the morning, and about 1630 that evening we faintly heard a call from him on the radio, saying that he had 24,000 gallons of fuel and he was trying to find us. We started making final preparations for the attack on the airfield, and the fuel got to us about midnight."

The next objective is a large enemy airfield near the Euphrates River, called Jalibah. It is normally the home of enemy fighters. Aerial photographs reveal many air defense artillery positions around the field, lots of bunkers and fortifications, and indications that the place is guarded heavily. Lieutenant Colonel Barrett:

"My battalion was to be the main effort, sweeping across the runways and through all the buildings and bunkers on the north side. For that I decided to put all four of my companies on line, giving me the maximum amount of firepower, go across in strength, then send units back to secure it in detail.

"Despite 50 mile per hour winds and visibilities that were sometimes down to about nothing—collecting the task force from a defensive posture oriented to the east, and posturing them in an attack formation oriented to the north in this driving storm at three in the morning was a challenge! But we did it and got into position to attack.

"The artillery prep started about 0500, and lasted an hour. Four battalions of artillery fired, two 155 mm., an 8-inch battalion, and a battalion of MLRS [Multiple-Launch Rocket System]—it was the most awesome thing I've ever seen in my life! I couldn't imagine anything surviving it—although, as it turned out, plenty did—and when the artillery was over, the Air Force went in."

The MLRS is the star performer, each round scattering dozens of deadly submunitions, each able to kill a tank or soldiers in the open. Then A-10 Warthogs sweep in, strafing enemy armor on the objective with 30-mm. depleted-uranium slugs. Eight tanks are reported on fire on the airfield. Lieutenant Colonel Barrett:

"We were moving then, all three battalions in formation. We oriented on a radio tower, our turning point, and using a 'box' formation with two tank-heavy companies leading and the mechanized infantry back, we started the assault across the airfield. Then the two infantry companies came on line to the right of the tanks and we assaulted in that manner.

There were a lot of tank and Bradley engagements, we received indirect fire from mortars and artillery, small arms fire. We took out over 600 prisoners, 24 tanks, 60 air defense guns, and 25 aircraft, helicopters and fixed wing. It was a beautiful assault-shock, power, maneuver, all done just like the textbook says.

"The scouts went out and discovered a bunker complex that belonged to a commando brigade, the elite of the elite of the Republican Guard. One of my scouts went into a bunker and captured the commando brigade commander. While they were pulling him out of the bunker, the phone rang. So this nineteen year old scout went over and picked up the phone and announced to the Iraqi at the other end [paraphrasing the famous line from the movie *Poltergiest*] 'Weee're Heeere!' and hung up."

As the task force moves up, 4/64 armor finds an enemy tank column on the highway near the airfield, running for their lives. Forty T-72s tanks are destroyed in a brief fight.

The attack on the airfield kicks off at daylight. Part of the force over-watches and provides covering fire while the rest sweeps across the complex, destroying everything of military value to the enemy. One of the over-watching tank commanders says, "We basically just sat there and blew things up. It was a

Although this Iraqi tank looks intact from the outside, it is completely burned out on the inside. USMC

case of overwhelming combat power. It was incredible!"

For the tanks preparing to sweep across the objective, the perspective is different, says Sergeant Haynes: "We moved up to the fence and I could see the whole battalion on line. Then the tanks started busting down the fence and I told the crew, 'Let's go for it!' We moved out, firing in sector." They discover an airplane missed by the preparatory attacks. Four tanks fire on it at virtually the same moment and it disappears in a cloud of scrap metal. They shift their fire to a large command bunker and for a moment it receives a barrage from tank main guns and Bradley 25-mm. white phosphorous rounds. Tracers from scattered enemy defenders mix with the tracers of the attackers in a daylight fireworks display.

Three Bradleys are hit by tank fire, killing two crewmen and injuring others. One of the Bradleys is driven off, the others allowed to burn. The task force drives on, firing into bunkers which begin to erupt from secondary explosions as the stockpiles of ammunition and explosives inside catch fire.

VII Corps

The Desert Rats, along with the entire British 1st Armoured Division, blast up into Iraq, Union Jacks flying from antennas, overwhelming the defenders.

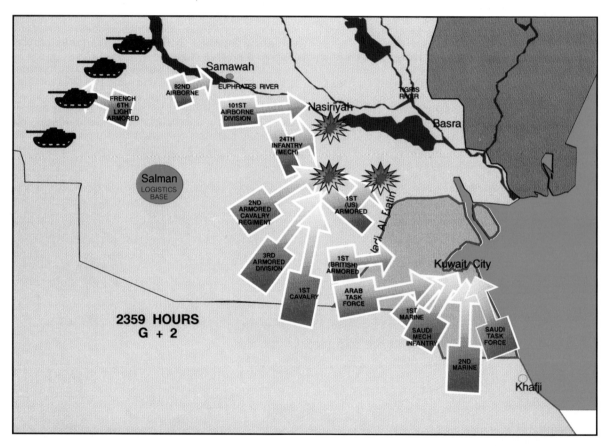

Midnight, three days into the land campaign, finds Kuwait City in the grasp of Arab and Marine units; XVIII and VII corps are rapidly rolling up the Iraqi units to the west. A mad dash by Iraqi units in Kuwait to escape the trap is cut off by ground and air attacks and by the Euphrates River. Elements of the Marine amphibious force off shore are finally permitted to come across the beach.

The British have the same problems with the flood of prisoners as do the other forces, but they're sometimes more polite than the Americans.

One of the Desert Rats offers tea to a captive. The Iraqi accepts it, but begins to cry.

The British are all proud volunteers, as are the American marines and soldiers, but they come from a longer tradition that their coalition partners find inspiring. British paratroop training makes the American version look like kindergarten. British troops are regarded with tremendous respect by their American comrades for their superior training, traditions and experience both in the Falklands and Northern Ireland.

And the Challenger and Chieftain tanks used by the British are as capable as the Abrams. Their Chobham laminate armor is highly effective against the anti-tank rounds fired at them. Some are hit by enemy main guns—and the noise is terriffic—but the armor does its duty.

The British dash is frantic, and ocassionally full of surprises. At one point the advance is led by an agressive artillery battery whose proper place in the procession is far to the rear. The British, like the Americans, encounter their countrymen who are EPWs, forced to serve in the Iraqi army. They are startled by the horrible condition of the prisoners, by the lack of care the enemy leaders have provided their men. When one group of several hundred prisioners are given a quantity of food, the officers consume it and the soldiers get none.

1st Cavalry

While the XVIII and VII corps divisions have been racing up to the Euphrates River and are now far to the north, ready to hit the Republican Guards, the 1st Cavalry has been busy back at the border. For weeks they've been poking a stick in the tiger's cage. They've been left behind by the big advance, and now they're pretty much alone, right where they started so long ago. But on day three, the big boss decides it's time to let them in on the fun.

At 0400 the brigade gets a warning order to prepare to move east, attack along the east side of the wadi and into Kuwait City. The battalions are ready to go, oriented to the east and ready to move. At 0800 they get the order: sorry, guys, change of mission. Turn around, move *west* and follow the 1st Infantry Division through their breach. Get to the Euphrates River valley ASAP. Everybody does an about-face, and the division moves out along Tapline Road toward the west. The Cav refuels at noon, is through the breach at midnight and jams.

Sitrep, Day Three

Seventy-two hours into the campaign, the enemy forces are nearly ejected from Kuwait, but they still hold Kuwait City. Most Iraqi units have either been destroyed or are running for their lives from the trap. XVIII Corps is only twenty-five miles to the west of Basra, but has finally confronted the Republican Guards. There have been occasional battles, but the allied combined arms tactics have easily prevailed. Casualties remain far lower than anyone hoped possible.

Even so, Sgt. Gary Streeter, a forty-year-old career soldier with the 1st Infantry Division, Big Red One, dies when his UH–60 Black Hawk helicopter is hit by ground fire. S. Sgt. Harold Witzke is dead, too, killed storming a bunker in Kuwait. Capt. Mario Fajardo dies leading his company through a minefield. Mines kill S. Sgt. Michael Harris, Cpl. Phillip Mobley, 1st Lt. Tery Plunk and Sp. Cindy Beaudin who go to help a wounded soldier and die in the attempt.

Chapter 6

27 February: G Plus 3

Day four, 0300, 197th Infantry: The 1/18 task force halts at a pipeline that is called Phase Line Normandy on the battle maps. Dirt has been pushed up on the pipe to form a large berm. The vehicles are nearly out of gas and begin refueling before the attack, waiting for the rest of the force to catch up.

In the meantime, though, it is time for the scouts to earn their pay, snooping forward. Two companies poke gun tubes across the berm, and the scouts are sent forward with the rest of the task force overwatching them. The scouts get across and into trouble. There are bunkers, equipment, and enemy soldiers everywhere, they report. They tippytoe through the night, a mile or so forward, to an eight-lane highway. A huge berm bars the way, they radio back.

Marines, Day Four

Task Force Shepherd gets tasked to take Kuwait International with Task Force Papa Bear about midnight. The commanders conspire on the radio, then move out onto a highway at about 0300 and drive up the road. They move to the southern gate to the airfield. A few diehards launch occasional Sagger missiles and machine gun fire at the force, but none hit. More damage is done by the rough terrain when they leave the road—several of the Humvees get flat tires.

Five fences bar the way, they're cut and Shepherd and Papa Bear sweep across the runway at about 0700. The enemy has mostly evaporated. The place is deserted, and the marines finally park at about 0745. The Iraqi flag is hauled down from the airport flag

Lt. Thomas Blackstock, Jr., Bravo Company, 27th Engineer Battalion, celebrates the taking of Salman airfield, Iraq, on G Plus 3. Kirby Lee Vaughn

pole and a Kuwaiti flag and a Marine Corps flag, grimy from exposure to oil smoke, are hoisted in its place. The airport is secured. Task Force Shepherd, for the first time in four days, rests. In a hangar the marines flop down on their mats and sleep for most of the next twenty-four hours.

The 2nd Marine Division's positions to the west are all tied in nice and tight, and marines are dug in on Mutla Ridge, overlooking the capital. The blockade of Kuwait City is air tight, and the stage is set for the liberation of the town. Kuwaiti resistance forces show up at the command post and the marines prepare to pass the Arab units through the lines into the city.

1st Cavalry

At 0400 on G Plus 3, 2nd Brigade, with the rest of the 1st Cavalry, refuels deep in Iraq. At 0600 they're moving again, an entire division in attack formation, twenty kilometers across and ten deep, sweeping up toward Basra and the Republican Guards at a steady twenty kilometers per hour. At noon the brigade stops to refuel, but by 1300 is moving again. Two hours later they drive across the top of Kuwait toward the Basra pocket where Republican Guard units are caught in the trap of AirLand Battle.

Piglet Saves the Day

One of the important missions involved in liberating Kuwait City will be the recapture of the American embassy. The planners expect this to be a major problem and dedicate considerable resources to prepare. A large special operations team, possibly including Delta Force, SEAL, Force Recon, Green Berets and special operations aviation units have rehearsed the take-down mission for weeks. It will be one of those dramatic, elaborate, helicopter insertions. The teams

An M1 Abrams on the move, making smoke. Department of Defense

An abandoned Iraqi APC at Salman airfield. Kirby Lee Vaughn

will "fast rope" onto the roof, clear the buildings room-by-room in the grand John Wayne tradition just as the Arab forces liberate the city. It is a big deal. But while they're getting ready for their big moment of glory, some young marines are going to steal it from them.

Prior to G Day, several Marine Force Recon teams—Piglet, High Tech and American Beauty—prowl the border area below Kuwait, providing intel on the opposing force. But on 23 February they are pretty much out of a job. The teams are all ratty looking (a Marine Corps combat tradition) and, with nothing to do, start to freelance, looking for adventure.

Piglet is commanded by Lt. Brian Knowles who is twenty-two. Team Piglet is intercepted by an American news team that includes a female reporter. She and Knowles snack on fruit juice and cookies while they drive north. It doesn't take long before Piglet and company are on the outskirts of the as-yet-unliberated Kuwait City. The reporter and Knowles decide to enter the city, and off they go. The news team is reduced to a cameraman and a print reporter, who hop in the vehicle with Knowles, and off they go.

Piglet bumps into some Kuwaiti resistance fighters and they stop to chat. "How do you get to the American embassy?" Knowles wants to know. They get directions and off they go with nobody to stop them and soon arrive. The place is deserted, but intact. The lieutenant sets up his satcom radio, calls back to his unit to let them know the American embassy is safe and sound. Come and get it!

Meanwhile, somewhere off shore, the large force that has prepared so long and hard for the rescue mission is applying its makeup for the big date. These guys are so serious they probably camouflage their teeth. And, about the time they are supposed to climb into the helicopters for their date with history, Knowles is chatting on the phone with his Force Recon compadres, telling them not to bother with the big raid.

The Piglet report gets quickly passed all the way to CENTCOM headquarters where somebody blows a gasket. "Tell him to get his ass out of there!" The whole special ops mission, with all its planning and potential for legend, evaporates. But it is too late, the embassy is secured a day before the Arab forces enter the city—by one young Marine officer and a couple of reporters. Marine public affairs strikes again!

Outside the city, the Arab task forces start to smell victory. Guns are fired into the air, soldiers start yelling happily, and they charge up the coast and in from the west. "It was like the liberation of Paris during World War II," the Marine liaison officer with

Even dug-in Iraqi armor was quickly destroyed by the swift-moving allied assault. USN

A Multiple-Launch Rocket System cuts one loose. These rockets are unguided, like artillery, but accurate and lethal. The warheads contain dozens of submunitions that are scattered across a wide area, effective against both vehicles and people. US Army

them says. Any opposition of any kind produces an immediate response from the Arabs: they all start shooting in all directions with whatever weapon is handy.

Liberation

Although the fighting continues in places, Kuwait City erupts in joy as the Kuwaiti and Saudi units rumble into town. The destruction is terrible, but the citizens turn out to greet their liberators with overpowering gratitude. The mother of all celebrations begins for the Kuwaitis.

The American reaction is more subdued. Most of the soldiers and marines are glad to find themselves alive and well at the end of the battle. The gratitude of the Kuwaitis is almost overwhelming. Back in the dark days of autumn, back when the issues were less clear, the soldiers and marines had heard the predictions about what would happen if the United States became involved in a Middle East conflict; it was a no-win situation, some said. Thousands of Americans would die, others predicted. A shooting war would split the country, according to other experts. According to the papers, the equipment and the people in the armed forces were neither effective nor reliable.

As the fighting stops and people have a chance to rest, relax and sleep, they thank each other in many ways. Near the Kuwait International Airport, amid the scattered debris of battle and occupation, four members of the 1st Marine Division Band approach their battalion commander. None has played any instrument except an M–16 rifle for over two months. Bandsmen normally process POWs in combat, and these four were as tired, dirty, scruffy and ragged as any grunt. But they came to attention before the commander and, without accompaniment, sang for him "The Star Spangled Banner." He cried. So did they.

Charlie Company, 1st Battalion, 7th Marines finally gets a casualty just outside Kuwait City. The Arab liberators celebrate their victory by firing personal weapons into the air, and one of the bullets comes down on the arm of a young marine watching the party. "You could have done more damage by throwing a sharp rock at him," one of his mates says.

For 1st Battalion, 7th Marines, the war is over. They mount up and drive through the freshly liberated city on the way back to Saudi Arabia, flags flying,

Inside an MLRS fire-control center, coordinates are punched into the fire-control computer. Hans Halberstadt

Global Positioning System

Operation Desert Storm involved the movement of hundreds of thousands of people, thousands of vehicles and hundreds of supporting aircraft across a featureless desert, day and night, in blowing sand, rain, fog and the smoke of six hundred burning oil wells. The ability of the task forces to navigate under such conditions was a minor miracle of high technology, a little device that can fit in a pocket called Global Positioning System (GPS). The device receives information from a satellite that displays the location of the receiver to within about fifteen feet.

Virtually everyone interviewed for this book raved about GPS as the one, crucial piece of technology in the campaign. Using it, platoon leaders could tell where they were, where they had to go. Tanks could link up with their fuel tankers in the middle of the night. GPS eliminated a lot of the natural confusion of maneuver warfare, speeding the attack, avoiding costly mistakes.

The comments of a company commander from the 82nd Airborne are typical: "GPS was a life saver! We only had one in the company, and I had it. Throughout the entire operation I could call out grids, tell people how to move, tell them exactly where we were. There is no other way to accomplish the mission we did without GPS."

Magellan GPS 1000. The Global Positioning System technology was clearly one of the war winners. Virtually all units had these little hand-held devices, and all raved about them. With visibility nearly zero, with no terrain features to provide reference, the tank crews and their commanders still knew exactly where they were at all times, to within a few feet. This information was used to coordinate fire, movements, get fuel to thirsty vehicles and tell friendly units from enemy. The map was used by Staff Sergeant Haynes of the 24th Infantry Division. Hans Halberstadt

to the cheers of the Kuwaitis who've survived the occupation. One of the little American flags comes loose from an antenna and falls in the dirt by the roadside; an elderly lady scoops it up, clutches it tightly and kisses it. She is crying.

Up north, the battle continues into the surreal night of day four, toward the climactic battle everyone expects on day five.

The Desert Rats and British 1st Armoured continue the charge around the Wadi Al Batin, press into Kuwait to the west of Kuwait City. Cpl. Pete Woolson, gunner on a Challenger tank named *Die Hard*, fires on an armored personnel carrrier. It comes apart, he says, like tin foil.

Eighteen British soldiers have been killed and fifty injured. A full half of the deaths are from a Maverick missile shot by an American A-10. The British, with their tradition of battlefield discipline, properly wonder about the battlefield discipline of their American allies.

The ability to keep the tanks resupplied was vital to the allied advance. Fuel tankers like this 5,000-gallon tanker often appeared just when the tanks needed them most. US Army

Humvees scout for Iraqi positions in the desert. Department of Defense

A destroyed Iraqi T–55 tank. From the outside all that may be visible is the small hole where the long-rod penetrator punched through the armor; inside, nothing is left intact. USN

More evidence of the 1st British Armoured Division's passing. This one was killed by the 7th Brigade, Royal Scots. The British leave a battlefield tidy of everything except enemy equipment, which they traditionally disassemble in violent ways. USN

On G Plus 3, Marine LAVs advance through Kuwait.
USMC

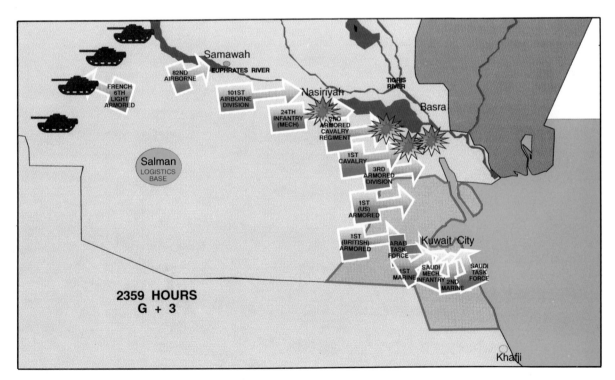

Midnight of the fourth day of ground combat finds most of the enemy forces out of action. Those still fighting are mostly Republican Guards, and they're trying to make a fighting withdrawal across the Euphrates River. But their communications are nearly destroyed, and they only succeed in driving themselves deeper into the trap. Kuwait City has been taken and the heavily armored divisions are preparing to sieze Basra.

Chapter 7

28 February: G Plus 4

On G Plus 4, the jaws of the vise are squeezing hard on the Republican Guards. For four days the combined forces of Britain, France, and the United States have been chasing the heavy formations of the Republican Guards, the real heart of Iraq's ability to wage war. For four days, the Guard has been pounded, pushed, and abraded. In the early hours of the fifth day, the soldiers and commanders from XVIII Corps face east and prepare for the battle the enemy has avoided thus far. They are trapped between the Euphrates River and the combined combat powers of XVIII and VII Corps, closing in for the kill.

In the early hours of 28 February, Republican Guards are reported in strength, and moving near the city of Basra, only a few miles from where the 24th Infantry has paused to refuel and resupply with ammunition. The mission for them will be to attack these forces. The battle should be intense.

All night the artillery supporting the attack fires over the heads of the lead elements.

One brigade of Iraqis tires of the pounding and takes to the highway in order to confront their tormentors. The force rolls down Highway Eight, only to be engaged by Apache helicopters and MLRS batteries. The Apaches destroy the lead vehicles with Hellfire missiles, blocking the formation. Then MLRS drops thousands of bomblets on the tanks, trucks and personnel carriers. A few break out and get to within 2,500 meters of 2/7 Battalion who engaged them from their flank. More than 180 enemy armored vehicles

The ammunition cooks off in an Iraqi tank after a direct hit from one of the British 1st Armoured Division's Chieftain or Challenger tanks. USN

were destroyed in the engagement, plus many more thin-skinned trucks and other vehicles.

The battalions don't get to rest, though. There is still the attack to launch in the morning. It has been ninety-six hours of nonstop tension for most of the soldiers, and all are short on sleep. Most have been gutting it out till now, but the pace and pressure start to catch up. Captain Sutherland tries to make notes while listening to his operations order for the attack on Basra, but falls asleep, his pen marking a straight line across the paper.

His battalion commander, Lieutenant Colonel Barrett, is still somehow awake. So are the drivers from the support platoon who've worked their magic again, getting fuel to the tanks and Bradleys just as they go dry. This time, though, they refuel under fire from the enemy.

Lieutenant Colonel Barrett: "My Support Platoon leader once again found fuel, and brought it forward. I don't know where he found the fuel, because we were moving so much faster than we'd been programmed. Under artillery fire, he refueled the battalion! Fourteen fuel trucks, each carrying 2,400 gallons moving around in the dark, and anytime an artillery round could blow them sky high. It was a rather hairy night, but we had to get the fuel in order to attack the next day. . .

"That was the night I was most scared. Artillery started coming in about 500 meters in front of my position. Another unit was receiving air bursts directly over their position.

"This was the exciting night. We were getting reports that we were catching up to the Republican Guards. There were reports of massive formations of BMPs and T-72s, thirty kilometers away from us . . . then that they turned our way. It was THE armor battle that everybody had been expecting.

107

"We got the warning order that night, and I started going through the map sheets: there's the city of Basra, and Basra International Airport; that was our mission for the next day! It was a real tense night! The artillery prep was the biggest we'd ever seen; it was awesome.

"The battalion lined up at four in the morning to get ready to kick off the attack. And about an hour later we got the word that there was going to be a cease fire. We were all real happy about that!"

Lieutenant Colonel Barrett: "We had about four hours sleep the first night, two the second, two hours the night of the 26th, none the night of the 27th . . . we were pretty tired. But we geared up for the attack the next morning, into Basra, the artillery prep went in at 0500, we were at REDCON ONE [the highest state of readiness], engines running and ready to go. When the prep was over I got a call: 'Do not move. Cease fire has been put into effect.' And that was pretty much it."

At daylight the units set up defensive positions and sit tight to see what happens.

An enemy truck arrives to confront the scouts, and a fire fight develops. One of the over-watching tanks kills the first truck, then another arrives, full of enemy soldiers. These don't feel like surrendering. One fires on the scouts with his AK-47, and the battle is on. This time the scouts have to fight their own little war, and two scouts are hit. The scout platoon leader fires his M203 grenade launcher into the cab of the truck, hitting the driver squarely in the face—but the range is so close that the warhead hasn't armed and doesn't explode. The driver dies anyway. But it takes machine gun fire to kill the other enemy soldiers.

The scouts extract their wounded while the guns of the task force, 400 meters away, fire their M19 grenade launchers and heavy machine guns in support. The 3/69 Battalion is moving forward when the scouts become engaged, and the brigade commander sends them off to take the objective. They find three places to cross the pipeline, get inside, and spread out on line.

The attack kicks off and soon finds itself in a huge complex of bunkers, equipment and enemy. Although told the area is clear of friendly forces, the scouts are still in the neighborhood, and one tank lases the scout vehicle, burning out the platoon leader's night vision goggles that saved him from blindness.

Enemy trucks start moving toward the force and are engaged by tanks firing HEAT rounds. The battalion kicks open a beehive. Through the thermal sights and night vision devices enemy soldiers are seen running in all directions. Green tracers from enemy machine guns float through the night back at the attackers. Firing is intense, coming from all directions. The Mk. 19 machine guns are used to deadly effect, with heavy .50-cal. machine guns, TOW missiles, 20-mm. cannons from the Bradleys, and main tank gun rounds seeking targets.

The task force blasts across objective area Utah, zigging around burning vehicles and bunkers. "It was amazing how well these guys were dug in. They had equipment, material, weapons." The bunkers are stuffed with ammunition. "We were just lucky we didn't fire into those bunkers," a sergeant says with a laugh. "We would have wiped out a company of our own guys with the secondary explosions!" Sunrise reveals a battlefield littered with enemy equipment, discarded in panic. Later, they begin coming in to surrender.

The prisoners are scared, but desperation drives them in. Their leaders have told them that the Americans will feed them, give them water, then kill them. They get food and water and get to live, too.

One platoon gets into a fire fight with an enemy unit at pointblank range when they bump into a truckload of Iraqi infantry escorting a staff car. In the staff car is a two-star general, and the little convoy drives into a road block and starts shooting. A squad leader fires his M203 into the truck cab. The 70-mm. round hits the driver in the face, killing him without exploding.

Automatic weapons fire goes in both directions, green tracers mixed with red. Thirteen enemy go down. The firing stops, and one squad provides security while another starts searching the wounded enemy. The enemy general is prone on the ground, but produces a pistol, aims at the back of one of the troops. A burst from a machine gun kills the general.

Elsewhere on the battlefield, troopers are clearing and securing bunkers and enemy positions. There is an old, burned-out BMP that had been shot up previously and seems to be abandoned. But while walking away the fire team is shot at from the rusting vehicle. They fire an AT-4 antitank rocket from eighty meters, but the warhead bounces off, much to the amazement and disgust of the soldiers. A tank crew comes to the rescue, firing a HEAT round into the BMP and taking it apart.

Tallil air base is to the west, a contingency target for the brigade and still untouched by the ground assault. Two tank teams, one team of infantry and an artillery battery are tasked to mount a raid on Tallil while the rest of the brigade pauses. The airfield is surrounded by a berm nearly thirty feet high, too big to easily breach. So the attack goes around and through the front gate. Once inside, the raiders sweep across the field, killing a tank. And then, under camouflage nets they find many enemy fighter aircraft, fueled and armed. One after another they explode from tank HEAT rounds.

But the field is well defended with heavy machine guns, RPGs, SA-60 missiles and plenty of enemy soldiers not ready to quit. After shooting up the place the tanks head for the exit. One of the M1s is hit and disabled. The crew is extracted safely and the tank left behind, but not before it is destroyed by the task force commander who fires two rounds into it. The first bounces off, the second penetrates and sets it on fire. The force dashes back thirty kilometers to the rest of the brigade in time to join the next attack. It kicks off at 1600. The terrain is still causing problems. On the attack several vehicles get embedded in mud and can't be extracted. The problem is complicated by enemy missile and machine gun fire. Two tanks and two armored personnel carriers are destroyed and discarded.

This unfortunate Iraqi T-55 was caught and destroyed by the US Air Force at the Multa Pass, north of Kuwait City. USAF/T. Sgt. Heimer

Three hundred miles deep into Iraq, the afternoon of the fourth day, the 24th Infantry Division and the 197th Brigade turn to the east, down the road to Basra. It is a surreal road race, hundreds of tanks, armored personnel carriers, and supporting vehicles dashing into the gathering night, as fast as they can go. For the M1 tanks, that's 40 to 50 mph; they're finally asked to slow down to let the supporting vehicles catch up. Enemy positions fire at them, being engaged in return. The road is lit by the fires of burning enemy bunkers and vehicles that have made the error of shooting at the parade. But the task force continues the rush, finally halting just to the west of Basra, ready to attack in the morning. Ahead—squirming off in the distance—is the remnant of the Republican Guards.

The road between Basra and Kuwait City was secured by British in the early hours of day three, preventing the Republican Guards' escape. All day, armored units have been closing with the Republican Guards survivors, still willing to shoot at coalition units.

Blocked on the west, south, and east, the Iraqi units frantically try to escape to the north. Some find bridges still standing and enemy engineers manage to ferry some across. The XVIII Corps commander, General Luck, tasks the 101st Airborne with another blocking mission, this one far to the east, north of Basra where the battle maps say Engagement Area Thomas.

Apache helicopters are sent out to execute the mission, staging out of a forward arm and refuel point (FARP) called Viper. They, and the OH-58D Kiowa scout helicopters are the only ones able to see and shoot effectively through the dense smoke that now covers the battlefield. They arrive to block the road, find it crawling with enemy convoys of tanks, trucks, personnel carriers, self-propelled artillery—anything the enemy has left intact and is able to move north is making a break for Baghdad.

Hellfire missiles streak toward the lead vehicles. Fireballs 100 meters across engulf the targets. One after another, the enemy armor explodes. Enemy soldiers break from the road, seek shelter in the adjoining swamps. One group will wave white flags while nearby one diehard will blast away with a machine gun.

Hovering low and shooting, the helicopters encounter a new hazard. Iraqis desperate to surrender try to grab the skids and landing gear. By 1630 the road is hopelessly blocked and the helicopters are pulled back to Viper.

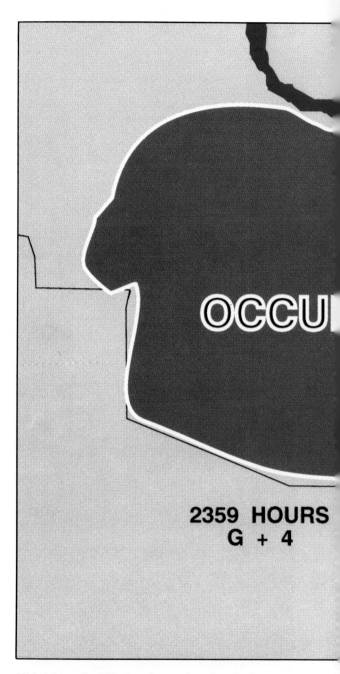

2359 HOURS G + 4

Midnight on the fifth day of ground combat finds a cease fire in place, but there's still plenty of shooting. Scattered enemy units still choose to fight, and some still think Iraq has been victorious. Some Republican Guard units

h

ES RIVER

TIGRIS
RIVER

Nasiriyah

Basra

D IRAQ

Kuwait City

Khafji

*have survived and are still attempting to get across the
Euphrates. Most of the coalition forces are finally able to
stay in one place for a few hours and get some sleep.*

AH–64 Apache Attack Helicopter

The AH–64 Apache helicopter is another system that helped win the battle, and like so many of the other critical weapons of the war, the Apache had been criticized for years.

Its job is the attack mission, part of the little, organic air force the Army relies on in combat. It carries Hellfire missiles to deal with heavy armor, a 25-mm. gun and 70-mm. rockets for lighter targets—troops and trucks—in the open. The

Apache pilot Maj. Rick Rife of the 1st Cav wears a $10,000 custom helmet, complete with television. Sensors on the bulkhead can "read" the helmet's exact orientation, permitting Major Rife to shoot at targets merely by looking at them and keying a switch on his cyclic control. Hans Halberstadt

guns are part of a complicated, expensive fire control system that is operated by the copilot-gunner sitting in the front seat. He is primarily responsible for shooting, the pilot in back is primarily in charge of flying the helicopter and navigation across the battlefield. They both need to be good because they work at night, flying 150 mph across the terrain, just above the surface.

The Apache proved the skeptics wrong from the first moments of the war, with the attack on the radar installations in western Iraq. They, rather than another system, were used because nothing else could sneak in undetected, engage from stand-off ranges, and keep shooting until the targets were all completely destroyed.

That mission was a natural for the Hellfire missile, eight of which are carried by the Apache. The missile is one of the smart munitions that were so effective. it uses a laser-seeker in its guidance system that permits a pilot in one air-craft, or a soldier on the ground, to mark a target with coded laser light. When launched, the missile seeks that special coded light and travels at high velocities across several miles to crash into the target. The result is a fireball that is often 100 meters across, the explosion of all the tank's ammunition.

It used to be a helicopter with a reputation for being unreliable, but readiness rates in excess of ninety percent were normal for all of the ground campaign.

Major Rife with the Apache's eyes: day TV, thermal imager, and laser rangefinder/designator. Hans Halberstadt

1st Cavalry

Midnight finds the 2nd Brigade preparing to move through the 1st Armored Division lines to attack the Republican Guards the next day. They've traveled 200 miles in twenty-four hours—without losing a tank or Bradley—perhaps the fastest movement of a brigade in the history of armored combat. The move has been made without benefit of a road, through minefields and rough terrain, and while refueling three times and the complete combat power is available and on line, ready to fight, the order to cease fire comes across the net. "The saddest day of my life," Colonel House says. "We had 'em! It was better than any training exercise I've ever been on. No casualties, no accidents, in a driving rainstorm when you couldn't see fifteen feet! The whole formation, moving together."

And that's where the cease fire finds the 2nd Brigade, 1st Cav, at 0800 on G Plus 4.

British 7th Brigade

Two hours before the cease fire time, 7th Brigade gets a mission: block the road north from Kuwait City—now! With friendly forces nearby the risk of friendly fire has never been greater. Visibility drops as the task forces approach the city and its burning oil fields, but the British secure the road. There is no escape for any Iraqi forces still mobile in southern Kuwait.

At the cease fire, they've come 150 miles in sixty-eight hours, fighting six major battles en route. 7th Brigade has killed ninety enemy tanks, uncounted other armor and vehicles and captured over 3,000 prisoners. It cost the Brigade two dead and fifteen wounded.

They're still ready to fight, if need be. They've helped chase the Republican Guards and secure the center of Kuwait. It has been one of the best performances of the war, demonstrating again the excellence of British training, equipment, and particularly people in the profession of arms.

Cease Fire!

At 0800 local time, Wednesday 28 February 1991, by order of the president and commander in chief, all offensive combat operations are suspended.

The war is over.

There will be a lot of work to do, and there will be more casualties in the days ahead. But the objective of Desert Storm was to eject the Iraqis from Kuwait, and the objective has been accomplished. Coalition forces occupy a large portion of Iraq.

Forty-two Iraqi divisions were captured, destroyed, or rendered combat ineffective by the applied combat power of the coalition forces. Iraq has lost perhaps 100,000 battle deaths, another 150,000 captures, 3,700 tanks destroyed, 1,875 armored vehicles destroyed, 2,140 artillery pieces destroyed. Iraq's air force is reduced to insignificance. The nation's infrastructure—roads, bridges, power plants, communication facilities, airports—is a smoldering ruin.

It has taken six weeks of offensive operations, five for the air campaign, and less than one more on the ground. The American cost is seventy-nine deaths as a result of enemy action: twenty-three during the air campaign, twenty-eight in the unlucky Scud attack, another twenty-eight on the ground.

Task Force Shepherd's commander is invited to a dinner with Kuwaiti resistance leaders and taken to a school where he accepts thanks on behalf of his marines. In return he gives a Marine Corps flag to the school. It is accepted with the pledge that it will forever fly beside the Kuwaiti flag.

Marine Capt. Joseph Molofsky sits with the Arab officers in the Saudi brigade commander's tent. It is time for the units from Qatar to depart, and they are sitting on carpets, eating sweets brought as a gift from the Qatar commander. A fire burns on the hearth in the center of the tent. General Myatt, commander of the 1st Marine Division, has sent Colonel Turkey a note of thanks for his bold counterattack on Khafji and the rescue of the two Marine recon teams. Colonel Turkey reads the note aloud, in English, to the Arab officers in attendance. Carefully replacing the letter in its envelope, the Saudi commander tells the other Arab commanders, "General Myatt has congratulated us for our performance in the battle of Khafji, and he has thanked us for the rescue of the Marine reconnaissance teams trapped there. I am pleased that the general has sent me this letter." He turns to Captain Molofsky, and continues, "But that's not necessary. We know that, had it been Saudi reconnaissance teams trapped in the city, Marines would have gone up there to rescue them as we did. And the reason for that is that now we are brothers. We have fought together, and that means a lot."

Chapter 8

Aftermath

Throughout the campaign it has been obvious that the Iraqi forces have communications problems. Their problems persist after the cease fire; some surviving units think Iraq has won the war. Others think they can still offer resistance. Although offensive operations stop on 27 February, defensive engagements continue for days. Two of the most dramatic take place on Saturday, G Plus 7.

A column of 140 enemy armored vehicles trying to escape encounters an element of the 24th Infantry Division and opens fire. The response comes from 120-mm. tank main guns, TOW missiles from the ground, and Hellfire missiles from the air. They lose sixty tanks and APCs destroyed and eighty captured.

Also on Saturday, 2 March (G Plus 7), Iraqi and American armor meet, this time at the little town of Safwan, Iraq, across the border from Kuwait. The meeting is to prepare for the conference that will formalize the cease fire. After a 250-mile race across southern Iraq, the 2nd and 4th battalions of the 37th Armored Brigade of the Big Red One rumble into an assembly area south of town to meet the defeated enemy. It is an extremely strange meeting. The Iraqi commanders believe they are there to accept the surrender of the coalition commanders, that the Republican Guards have the allied forces surrounded and defeated. Tanks are gun-tube to gun-tube in a standoff that lasts for quite a while. Said Lt. Col. Dave Marlin: "After some negotiations with the brigade commander and the assistant division commander, they were given an ultimatum to be out of town by a certain hour. And if that did not take place, they would be killed. The Iraqis stalled most of the day, then left in a big hurry, with us hot on their heels. We went through the town, clearing it, with the full intention of killing any remaining Iraqi forces."

Two days later, in a tent complex on an airfield nearby, the enemy commanders are delivered to a conference with General Schwarzkopf and other senior coalition leaders. But first, a little demonstration. Lieutenant Colonel Marlin's 2nd Battalion, 37th Armor is tasked to provide an escort service for the Iraqis. The battalion's biggest, toughest "animals" are selected to be the hosts. When the guests arrive, they are checked for weapons and sent in pairs to a waiting convoy of Humvees. Each of the Humvees has a big, muscular, mean-looking driver and a guard with a shotgun. The guard is bigger, meaner and even more muscular. They refuse to talk to the Iraqis. Once all are ready, the convoy moves off down the runway

On 10 March 1991, Bravo Company, 27th Engineer Battalion, holds a memorial service for their fallen comrades. Kirby Lee Vaughn

117

with two Bradleys leading and two M1 tanks trailing. At the end of the runway, as a demonstration, the two tanks accelerate up the sides of the convoy at full throttle, the final flourish of a campaign to ensure the enemy commanders have a good idea of what coalition combat power looks like close up—in case they didn't already know.

When the talks are over a few hours later, it is with complete agreement and acceptance of terms. The battles are over, the shooting stops, and the thoughts of half a million Americans, British, French, Saudi, Egyptian, Syrian, and all the others finally turn toward home.

Lessons Learned

There were a lot of war winners in Desert Storm. One certainly was the air campaign, which prepared the battlefield as air power has never done before. While air power didn't win the war alone, it made the winning far less costly than it might have been.

Another was the quality of the weapons coalition forces used. Despite many years of criticism of the complicated, expensive tanks, aircraft and missile systems, the technology used turned out to be effective, reliable and efficient.

Yet another was the quality of the people who participated. It's been said that the coalition forces could have traded weapons and equipment with the Iraqis and still defeated them, and that's probably true. The most impressive weapons were the young soldiers and marines, the young sergeants and lieutenants, who made the whole thing work. They did it on little sleep, little food, while being shot at, on a battlefield lit by fire and obscured by smoke and blowing sand. Much of the success of Desert Storm came from the way the armed forces have selected, trained and led the young people in the profession of arms.

And finally, the basic fighting doctrine that the planning staff used to design the operation was also a war winner. The doctrine is called AirLand Battle, an elegant philosophy that summarizes the way the American Army intends to fight.

American Army and Marine Corps Personnel Killed in Desert Storm

Andy Alaniz, US Army
Clarence Allen, US Marine Corps
Frank Allen, US Army
Tony Applegate, US Army
Steven Atherton, US Army
Stanley Bartusiak, US Army
Cindy Beaudoin, US Army
Lee Belas, US Army
Stephen Bentzlin, US Marine Corps
John Boliver, US Army
Joseph Bongiorni, US Army
John T. Boxler, US Army
Roger Brilinski, US Army
Tommy Butler, US Army
William Butts, US Army
Jason Carr, US Army
Ismael Catto, US Marine Corps
Beverly Clark, US Army
Melford Collins, US Army
Mark Connelly, US Army
A. Bradley Cooper, US Army
William Costen, US Army
Allen Craver, US Army
David Crumby, Jr., US Army
Michael Dailey, US Army
Roy Damian, Jr., US Army
Michael Daniels, US Army
Manuel Davila, US Army
Marty Davis, US Army
Luis Delgado, US Army
Young Dillon, US Army
David Douthit, US Army
Robert Dryer, US Army
Mario Fajardo, US Army
Steven Farnen, US Army
Eliseo Felix, US Marine Corps

Douglas Fielder, US Army
Michael Fitz, US Army
Phillip Garvey, US Army
Rolando Gelagneau, US Army
Kenneth Gentry, US Army
Robert Godfrey, US Army
Troy Gregory, US Marine Corps
Michael Harris, US Army
Jimmy D. Haws, US Army
James Hawthorne, US Marine Corps
Timothy Hill, US Army
Duane Hollen, Jr., US Army
Aaron Howard, US Army
John Wesley Hutto, US Army
Thomas Jenkins, US Marine Corps
Glen Jones, US Army
Phillip Jones, US Marine Corps
Jonathan Kamm, US Army
Anthony Kidd, US Army
Jerry King, US Army
David Kramer, US Army
Edwin Kutz, US Army
Cheryl LaBeau-O'Brien, US Army
Brian Lane, US Marine Corps
Michael Linderman, US Marine Corps
Joseph Lumpkins, US Marine Corps
Anthony Madison, US Army
Steven Mason, US Army
Christine Mayes, US Army
James McCoy, US Army
Jeff Middleton, US Army
James Miller, US Army
Michael Mills, US Army
Adrienne Mitchell, US Army
Phillip Mobley, US Army
Andrew Moller, US Army

Garett Mongrella, US Marine Corps
Candelario Montalvo, US Marine Corps
John Morgan, US Army
James Murray, Jr., US Army
Patbouvier Ortiz, US Army
Aaron Pack, US Marine Corps
William Palmer, US Army
Kenneth Perry, US Army
David Plasch, US Army
Terry Plunk, US Army
Christian Porter, US Marine Corps
Dodge Powell, US Army
Ronald Randazzo, US Army
Hal Reichle, US Army
Ronald Rennison, US Army
Scott Schroeder, US Marine Corps
Brian Scott, US Army
Timothy Shaw, US Army
Stephen Siko, US Army
Brian Simpson, US Army
Russell Smith, US Army
David Snyder, US Marine Corps
David Spellacy, US Marine Corps
Christopher Stephens, US Army

Dion Stephenson, US Marine Corps
Adrian Stokes, US Army
Thomas Stone, US Army
Gary Streeter, US Army
William Strehlow, US Army
George Swartzendruber, US Army
Robert Talley, US Army
James Tatum, US Army
Donaldson Tillar, US Army
Reginald Underwood, US Marine Corps
Roger Valentine, US Army
Robert Wade, US Army
James Waldron, US Marine Corps
Daniel Walker, US Marine Corps
Frank Walls, US Army
Troy Wedgewood, US Army
David M. Wieczorek, US Army
James Wilbourn, US Marine Corps
Jonathan Williams, US Army
Corey Winkle, US Army
Harold Witzke, US Army
Richard Wolverton, US Army
James Worthy, US Army
Thomas Zeugner, US Army

British Soldiers Killed in Desert Storm

Paul Peter Atkinson, Royal Fusiliers
David Clifford, Royal Military Police
Conrad Phillip Cole, Royal Fusiliers
Stephen Richard Crofts, Royal Corps of Transport
David Edwin Denbury, Royal Engineers
Neil Walker Duncan Donald, Queen's Own Highlanders
Michael James Dowling, Royal Electrical and Mechanical Engineers
Francis Carrington Evans, Royal Electrical and Mechanical Engineers
Alistair James Fogerty, Royal Ordnance Corps
Richard Gillespie, Royal Fusiliers
Thomas Haggerty, Royal Scots
Martin Ferguson, Queen's Own Highlanders

Terence William Hill, Royal Corps of Transport
Paul Patrick Keegan, Royal Artillery
James Scott Kingham, Royal Engineers
Donald James Kinnear, Royal Army Pay Corps
John William Lang, Queen's Own Highlanders
Kevin Leech, Royal Fusiliers
Jason Patrick McFadden, Royal Corps of Transport
Carl Moult, Staffordshire Regiment
Robert Robbins, Royal Corps of Transport
Richard Allen Royle, Royal Engineers
Stephen Timothy Satchell, Royal Fusiliers
Shaun Patrick Taylor, Staffordshire Regiment
Lee James Thompson, Royal Fusiliers
Alastair John Wright, Royal Engineers

Major US Commands Deployed

Army
1st Cavalry Division, Fort Hood, Texas
1st Infantry Division, Fort Riley, Kansas
3rd Armored Cavalry Regiment, Fort Bliss, Texas
82nd Airborne Division, Fort Bragg, North Carolina
101st Airborne Division, Fort Campbell, Kentucky
2nd Armored Division, Fort Hood, Texas

197th Infantry Brigade, Fort Benning, Georgia
24th Infantry Division, Fort Stewart, Georgia

Marines
1st Marine Division, Camp Pendleton, California
2nd Marine Division, Camp Lejune, North Carolina

Major British Commands Deployed

1st Armoured Division

7th Armoured Brigade
The Royal Scots Dragoon Guards
The Queen's Royal Irish Hussars
1st Bn, The Queen's Dragoon Guards
1st Bn, The Staffordshire Regiment
40th Field Regiment, Royal Artillery, (RA)
10th Air Defence Battery, RA
21st Engineer Regiment
207th Signals Squadron, Royal Corps of Signals
  (RCS)
654th Squadron, Army Air Corps (AAC)

4th Armoured Brigade
14th/20th King's Hussars
3rd Bn, The Royal Regiment of Fusiliers
1st Bn, The Royal Scots
2nd Field Regiment, RA
46th Air Defence Battery, RA
23rd Engineer Regiment
204th Signals Squadron
659th Squadron, AAC

Divisional assets
16th/5th, The Queen's Royal Lancers
32nd Heavy Regiment, RA
26th Field Regiment, RA
39th Heavy Regiment, RA
12th Air Defence Regiment, RA
32nd Armoured Engineer Regiment, Royal
  Engineers
4th Regiment, AAC
1st Armoured Division Transport Regiment, Royal
  Corps of Transport (RCT)
4th Armoured Division Transport Regiment, RCT

1st Armoured Division Field Ambulance, Royal
  Army Medical Corps (RAMC)
5th Armoured Division Field Ambulance, RAMC
3rd Ordnance Battalion, Royal Army Ordnance
  Corps (RAOC)
7th Armoured Workshop, Royal Electrical and
  Mechanical Engineers (REME)
11th Armoured Workshop, REME

Force Troops
205th General Hospital, RAMC
24th Air Mobile Field Ambulance, RAMC
22nd Field Hospital, RAMC
32nd Field Hospital, RAMC
33rd General Hospital, RAMC
Elements of 30th Signals Regiment, Royal Corps of
  Signals

Forward Maintenance Area
6th Armoured Workshop, REME
7th Aircraft Workshop, REME
6th Ordnance Group, RAOC

The Life Guards
9th/12th, Royal Lancers
17th/21st, Lancers
4th Royal Tank Regiment
1st Bn, The Grenadier Guards
1st Bn, Scots Guards
1st Bn, The Devonshire and Dorset Regiment
1st Bn, The Prince of Wales Own Regiment of
  Yorkshire
1st Bn, Queen's Own Royal Highlanders
1st Bn, The Royal Green Jackets

123

Nations Participating in Desert Shield/Storm

Argentina	Australia	Bahrain
Bangladesh	Belgium	Canada
Czechoslovakia	Denmark	Egypt
France	Germany	Greece
Italy	Kuwait	Morocco
Netherlands	New Zealand	Niger
Norway	Oman	Pakistan
Poland	Qatar	Saudi Arabia
Syria	Senegal	Spain
United Arab Emirates	United Kingdom	United States

Index

About the Author

Hans Halberstadt is a writer, photographer and film producer who lives in San Jose, California. Halberstadt spent three years in the US Army, including one year as a helicopter gunner in Vietnam. That experience resulted in an abiding interest in life-and-death issues that influences most of his projects. His previous books include *USCG: Always Ready*, *Airborne: Assault From the Sky* and *Green Berets: Unconventional Warriors*. He is currently working on future POWER Series books on the British Desert Rats and the Red Army.

Now from Motorbooks International, The POWER Series provides an in-depth look at the troops, weapon systems, ships, planes, machinery and missions of the world's modern military forces. From training to battle action, the top military units are detailed and illustrated with top quality color and black and white photography.

Available through book shops and specialty stores or direct. Call toll free 1-800-826-6600. From overseas 715-294-3345 or fax 715-294-4448

AIRBORNE: Assault from the Sky—
by Hans Halberstadt
America's front line parachute divisions

AIR GUARD: America's Flying Militia—
by George Hall
From the cockpit on their flying missions

ARMY AVIATION—by Hans Halberstadt
American power house; how it evolved, how it works

C-130: The Hercules—by M. E. Morris
Full technical and operations analysis on this sky truck

DESERT SHIELD: The Build-up; The Complete Story—by Robert F. Dorr
All the action leading up to Operation Desert Storm

DESERT STORM AIR WAR—
by Robert F. Dorr
Blow-by-blow account of the allied air force and naval air campaign to liberate Kuwait

DESERT STORM SEA WAR—
by Arnold Meisner
Sailor's-eye view of naval combat, including carrier air operations, during Desert Storm

GREEN BERETS: Unconventional Warriors—by Hans Halberstadt
"To liberate from oppression"

ISRAEL'S ARMY—by Samuel M. Katz
Inside this elite modern fighting force

ISRAEL'S AIR FORCE
by Samuel M. Katz
Inside the world's most combat-proven air force

MARINE AIR: First to Fight—
by John Trotti and George Hall
America's most versatile assault force

NTC: A Primer of Modern Mechanized Combat—by Hans Halberstadt
The US National (Tank and Helicopter) Training Center

STRIKE: US Naval Strike Warfare Center—
by John Joss and George Hall
US Navy's "Top Gun" for ground attack pilots

TANK ATTACK: A Primer of Modern Tank Warfare—
by Steven J. Zaloga and Michael Green
American tanks and tactics in the 1990s

TOP GUN: The Navy's Fighter Weapons School—by George Hall
The best of the best

USAFE: A Primer of Modern Air Combat in Europe—by Michael Skinner and George Hall
Ever alert in an ever-changing world

USAREUR: The United States Army in Europe—by Michael Skinner
Sister title to USAFE

More titles are constantly in preparation